MEDIEVAL LOGIC

MEDIEVAL LOGIC

An Outline of Its Development
from 1250 to c.1400

BY

PHILOTHEUS BOEHNER
O.F.M.

Wipf & Stock
PUBLISHERS
Eugene, Oregon

Wipf and Stock Publishers
199 W 8th Ave, Suite 3
Eugene, OR 97401

Medieval Logic
An Outline of Its Development from 1250 to c. 1400
By Boehner, Philotheus
ISBN 13: 978-1-55635-592-9
ISBN 10: 1-55635-592-0
Publication date 9/6/2007
Previously published by The University of Chicago Press, 1952

PREFACE

THIS ESSAY on the elements and the systems of scholastic logic does not pretend to fill in a lacuna. Rather it will show that there is a gap which ought to be filled in. Be that as it may, the principal objective of this work is to foster an understanding between modern and neo-scholastic logic. We are personally convinced that such an understanding between these powerful groups of modern philosophy is not only possible but highly desirable, not to say necessary, for the benefit of both.

A mediator is usually in a rather awkward position. Rarely does he succeed in pleasing both sides. The author appreciates that in his plea for the essentially formal character of scholastic logic he will meet with a certain suspicion from neo-scholastics. Likewise he realizes that modern logicians may expect more from this booklet than it is willing and able to offer. In any case, our intention is to convey an idea of genuine scholastic logic to neo-scholastics and modern logicians.

The bare outlines of this study were first published in the *Revista de la Universidad Nacional de Córdoba*, Año XXXI (1944), pp. 1599-1620, under the title: "El sistema de Lógica Escolástica". Even though expanded to about five times its original size, it treats of its subject at best in only a summary fashion. Needless to say, much more research will be required until it will be possible to write an accurate history of medieval logic. At present we are able to present only samples from this relatively unexplored field.

The author is much indebted to James McSweeny and Paul Purta, of Christ the King Seminary, and to Fathers Gabriel Buescher, O.F.M., and Allan Wolter, O.F.M., of the

Franciscan Institute, St. Bonaventure, N.Y., for reading
and editing the manuscript.

   It is a great satisfaction to us to be able to dedicate this
study to our friend and mentor, Étienne Gilson, recently ele-
vated to the distinctive rank of the Académie Française. It
was his counsel which first directed us to a thorough study
of Ockham's philosophy, a course which of necessity had to
lead into the midst of medieval logic, and, as our other
friend, Professor Scholz of the University of Münster, had
predicted years ago, into the field of modern logic as well.

                                                    P. B.

THE FRANCISCAN INSTITUTE
   ST. BONAVENTURE, N.Y.
        1950

CONTENTS

INTRODUCTION

THERE IS no scarcity of books on neo-scholastic logic. Yet despite their number, they differ little among themselves. Their common pattern and similar content readily create the impression that here at least is a science that has weathered the vicissitudes of two millennia and is as firm and solid today as it was when Aristotle first completed his *Organon*. Naturally individual textbooks will vary, but there is a sameness in their very differences, for their variations are always in points of minor detail, for the most part, in the mode of presentation or the length devoted to the treatment of a particular point in their common subject matter. And though they all claim to be "scholastic", it is not to the logic of such textbooks that we refer when we speak, in the following pages, of scholastic logic.

In fact, we even hesitate to call the logic of such textbooks "neo-scholastic", at least if this term be taken in its literal meaning. For this "logic" is in such a state as to provoke the criticism not only of modern non-scholastic logicians, but also of any neo-scholastic versed in the history of his own tradition. The former will deny that it is new; the latter that it is scholastic. At best the modern logician will charitably ignore it. At the worst, he will be tempted to excoriate what he mistakes for the scholastic or even the Aristotelian science and which he designates by that vague, ambiguous and even faulty title of "classical" or "traditional logic". But in either case, the modern logician is convinced that he has little or nothing to learn from the scholastics and that his own logic is essentially different and vastly superior to anything produced in the Middle Ages.

On the other hand, he may be interested in the wider

aspects of scholasticism, not merely as an historical curiosity but as a system that deserves to live for the sake of the positive contribution it can make to contemporary culture. If so, our logician will be grieved at the condition of "neoscholastic" logic. He will be painfully aware of its inability to measure up to the scholastic logic of the 13th and 14th centuries. He will realize that somewhere between the classical period of scholasticism and the 18th century scholastic logic has been watered down. Foreign elements have been assimilated and have displaced some of the most important logical contributions made by the scholastics. He must admit to his shame that modern logicians had to rediscover independently much that the scholastic tradition could and should have transmitted.

Unfortunately there are still neo-scholastic logicians—though happily their number is decreasing—who are convinced that their logic is genuinely scholastic and that it cannot be surpassed by anything that modern logic has to offer. They look askance at the latter's formalism. They are suspicious of its symbolic form. They are afraid of repeating the Cartesian experiment of mixing mathematical thinking with philosophical speculation. Their coldness and openly hostile attitude are not wholly without reason, since modern logic has made its most striking development not only in the hands of mathematicians, but also in the shadow of Positivism. Curiously enough, they seem to share with Kant the firm belief that logic has not progressed since the time of Aristotle.[1] Yet the history of their own tradition should dispel this illusion, for the history of scholastic logic alone gives ample proof of a decided advance beyond the Stagirite's logic. As to the association of modern logic with Positivism—which, incidentally, is by no means general—it is well to remember that the great Aquinas was not shocked at the strange bed-fellows truth might pick. Aristotle was a genuine pagan. Averroes, his most faithful com-

mentator, and Avicenna, the greatest metaphysician of
Arabic philosophy, were Mohammedans with a more or less
marked tendency towards Rationalism. St. Thomas learned
from all who had something to offer. And if some of our
neo-scholastics today had more of the Saint's spirit, we
would be spared the sorry spectacle of a war against
"modern innovations", particularly when these innovations embody certain insights and teachings of Aquinas
himself. Interesting to note is the fact that within the sphere
of neo-scholasticism, certain Catholic scholars of the War-
saw School of modern logic, like Salamucha, Bochenski,
O.P., and others, find no opposition between the teachings
of St. Thomas and other scholastics and the modern logic,
once the latter is divested of its positivistic interpretation.
Quite the contrary, they have discovered surprising simi-
larities, correspondences and even identical doctrines. This
is the school fathered by Lukasiewicz, one of the most
prominent pioneers of modern Logic.

For those who have more than a passing acquaintance
with modern logic, it is an accepted fact that this logic has
made tremendous strides forward. It is likewise a fact—and
one which current research continues to confirm—that these
new developments have deviated far less from the logic of
the 13th and 14th centuries than from that of our neo-
scholastic textbooks. This present study in the elements
and systems of scholastic logic should make this evident.
And while, in the space of this relatively short work, it is
impossible to do full justice to the subject of scholastic
logic, the several samples and selections we have made
should make it clear that it is far easier to compare modern
logic with that of the scholastics than with that of the neo-
scholastics. For, in the latter case, there is often no basis
for comparison.

Among the elements shared in varying degrees by genuinely scholastic logic and modern logic, there is one in

particular that brings them in close proximity and facilitates a comparison. It is the character of formality, conserved in a much purer form in scholastic logic than in its neo-scholastic counterpart. The real reason why certain neo-scholastics are averse to the "formalism" of modern logic is to be found precisely in the non-scholastic elements of their neo-scholastic logic.[2]

Before taking up the discussion of our principal problems, it is well to clarify the meaning of certain terms we shall use in the course of this study, and to indicate the symbolism we shall employ. This is necessary in view of the fact that even among modern logicians there is no commonly accepted symbolism. As to the meaning of terms outside the proper field of logic, still greater confusion reigns, for modern logicians are too often prone to forget their wonted exactness when it comes to historical facts.

By *neo-scholastic logic* we mean that presentation of logic found in current textbooks written by neo-scholastics for the use of ecclesiastical seminaries and similar institutions. As types, we mention the textbooks of Hickey, Esser, Maritain and Gredt.[3] In addition, we include under this term all presentations of logic similar to these works. Only occasionally shall we have occasion to refer to this logic in the pages that follow.

By *scholastic logic* we refer to the logic taught during the 13th, 14th and 15th centuries in the Latin Occident, which has come down to us in various compendia, commentaries and other writings. Only a small fraction of this logic is accessible in modern editions. The bulk still remains hidden in old editions, incunabula and manuscripts. For the sake of convenience, we have begun with the 13th century, though this does not imply that the logic of the 12th-century scholastics was of no importance. We have also excluded the work of Ramond Lull, since we have to confess we are not sufficiently familiar with his peculiar logic to deal with it adequately, though we suspect that it is much better than the usual evaluation by historians would lead us to believe.

By *Aristotelian logic* we understand the doctrines of Aristotle himself which are contained in the collection of his logical works known as the *Organon*. In this sense, Aristotelian logic is something quite different from scholastic, neo-scholastic or even Greek logic. Important as Aristotle's logic may be,[4] it cannot simply be identified with Greek logic as such. For the logic of the Stoics, which is at least of equal importance as that of Aristotle, differs in this, that the Stoics developed the hypothetical syllogism with a clear insight into the material implication and its theorems and were well aware of the basic rôle played by the propositional calculus. Indeed, of all the systems of ancient times the Stoic logic appears to have the clearest right to be called the forerunner of modern logic.[5] Because elements of this logic seem to have been incorporated in the works of the Aristotelian commentators, it seems best to confine the term "Aristotelian logic" precisely to the logic of the *Organon*.

In our treatment of this matter we shall avoid using the terms "classical" or "traditional logic" which are frequently employed by modern logicians. Just what modern logicians mean by these terms is difficult to say. At times it would seem that they are used to designate a vague combination of the system of Aristotle and that of the neo-scholastics, or even the neo-scholastic logic. At any rate, the terms are misleading, and if modern logicians designate as "classical" or "traditional logic" all systems that have preceded their own, then a great many of their statements are simply false.

By *modern logic* we mean that tremendous development which has found its most outstanding expression in the *Principia Mathematica* of Whitehead and Russell. This characterization, however, is not intended to be exclusive, but rather paradigmatical. Modern logic therefore would include all previous expositions of logic in the manner of the *Principia*. Such, for instance, is the Boolean Algebra, the works of Frege and Peano. Similarly, the term embraces all subsequent developments such as the poly-valued logics of Lukasiewicz and Post, or the logic of strict implication and modalities as advanced by Lewis-Langford and expanded by Carnap. This modern system is sometimes called "symbolic logic", "logistics" or "mathematical logic". It would seem preferable, however, to avoid the term "symbolic logic", since the use of symbols is not confined to modern logic. It has been in vogue since ancient times. Similarly, it would seem advisable to avoid the name "mathematical logic", at least if we understand by logic precisely that more basic science which underlies mathematics, and for that very reason stops short of mathematics.[6]

And finally, lest there be any misunderstanding, let us make clear at the outset that logic as we understand it is *formal*, that is to say, it studies the form or structure of inferences and their elements. Hence, to speak of "formal logic" is, in scholastic terminology, a *nugatio* or tautology. To speak of "material logic" is a simple contradiction. In this we are in harmony with the scholastic logicians, for scholastic logic too is interested only in the formality or structure of discourse. Hence it does not recognize the distinction of formal and material logic. However, *nomina sunt ad placitum instituentium*.

EXPLANATION OF SYMBOLS

The following symbolization will be employed in the subsequent discussion:

p, q, r Propositional variables. An instance of p is: Socrates is running; Socrates currit. Scholastics sometimes use the small letters, $a, b, c \ldots$

x, y, z Individual variables. An instance of x is: This individual, that individual, Socrates, Plato, etc. Scholastics again use the first letters of the alphabet.

f, g, h Predicate variables. An instance of f is: "Man, mortal".

$(x)f(x)$ Universal quantification. An instance of this is: "Every individual is good"; "Omne ens est bonum".

$(\exists x)f(x)$ Particular quantification. An instance of this is: "Some individual is good"; "Aliquod ens est bonum".

$f(x_1)$ Individual or singular quantifier. An instance of this would be: "This individual is good"; "Istud ens est bonum".

$\bar{p}$ A dash above a symbol signifies a negation of that symbol.

.   The dot between symbols indicates the conjunction "and", and signifies that both members of the conjunction are true.

v   The small v indicates the disjunction "or", and signifies that at least one member of the disjunction is true.

⊃   This symbol indicates "if-then", and signifies that it is not the case that the part before the symbol (the antecedent) is true and the part following the symbol (the consequent) is false.

≡   This symbol indicates an equivalence.

The use of other symbols, when necessary, will be explained in their context. We have retained the use of parentheses, since many of those who are interested in this discussion are more familiar with their use.

PART ONE

ELEMENTS OF SCHOLASTIC LOGIC

I

THE LEGACY OF SCHOLASTIC LOGIC

W E MAY safely describe the initial scholastic contribution to logical literature as a series of commentaries
and paraphrases on the logical treatises of Aristotle, Porphyry and Boethius. Omitting for simplicity's sake the
very important work done by Abelard and his school, we
may regard St. Albert's tracts on logic as a fair approxima-
tion of the total heritage bequeathed to the schoolmen of
the mid-13th century. To begin with St. Albert is admittedly arbitrary. But as we are still very much in the dark
regarding the logical literature which preceded or accom-
panied the vast encyclopedic work of Albert the Great, for
all practical purposes we are justified in starting with the
latter. As we know from his own words, the "Doctor ex-
pertus" intended to make readily accessible to his contem-
poraries in the Latin Occident all the scientific and
philosophic knowledge then available in the works of the
Greek, Arabian and Jewish philosophers.[7] The following list
represents his edited and unedited works on logic in which
he presents, sometimes in simple paraphrase, sometimes in
important digressions, what he considered the best in logical tradition. We have employed a somewhat schematic
method, indicating the volume and pages of the Vivès edition, if the work is to be found there, and adding a brief
description of its content.

(1) *De praedicabilibus* (Vol. I, pp. 1-143). This book represents in a more expanded form Porphyry's *Isagoge*
and therefore deals with the classification of concepts
on the basis of their mode of predication; namely,
genus, species, difference, property and accident.

(2) *De praedicamentis* (Vol. I, pp. 149-304). Following
Aristotle's tract on the *Categories*, Albert discusses the
highest predicates applicable to real things or individuals, namely, substance, quality, quantity, relation,
action, affection (passio), position, time, place and
state. General though our description of this tract be,
at least it indicates why the term "ens" or individual
or thing is not a category according to Aristotle, since
it is a subject in an eminent sense and not properly a
predicate. Albert prefaces his treatise on the categories
with an important introduction on univocal, equivocal
and denominative names and concludes with an equally
important discussion on oppositions, on motion and
rest, or the *Postpraedicamenta* as they were known to
the scholastics.

(3) *De sex principiis* (Vol. I, pp. 305-372). This deals with
the treatise, *Concerning the Six Principles*, in which
Gilbert de la Porée († 1154) develops the brief remarks
of Aristotle on the last six categories into an extended
treatise. It begins with a discussion on "form" and
closes with another on "more" and "less". To Gilbert
apparently we owe the crudely realistic interpretation
of such categories as "time", "place" and the like
which was adopted by some of the scholastics.

(4) *De divisione* (edited by P. de Loe under the title *Beati
Alberti Magni Commentarii in Librum Boethii de Divisione*, Bonn, 1913). Paraphrasing Boethius' work on
division, this treatise discusses the division of genus
into species, the whole into its parts, the spoken word
into its several meanings and the distinction of accidents on the basis of subjects, of subjects by reason of
accidents and accidents according to accidents.

(5) *Perihermenias* (Vol. I, pp. 373-457), a paraphrase on
Aristotle's tract on propositions which comprised two
books according to the medieval division. The first

book is an analysis of propositions into their elements, together with a discussion of truth or falsity as a property of propositions. The special problem of the truth or falsity of future contingent factual propositions is given due attention in the last portion of this book. The second book is chiefly concerned with the equivalence, conversion and opposition of both simple categorical and modal propositions.

(6) *Priora Analytica* (Vol. I, pp. 459-809) represents a paraphrase of the central portion of Aristotelian logic, which, as Scholz has pointed out,[8] is far richer and more interesting than any school logic limited to a discussion of Barbara, Celarent, etc., would lead one to suspect. Not only does Albert discuss the categorical syllogism which comprises factual propositions (mere de inesse), but following the lead of Aristotle and others devotes a lengthy discussion to the modal syllogism, composed of modal propositions, and the mixed syllogism, comprising a factual and modal premiss. The second book is devoted mainly to the "potency" of the syllogism, that is, to an evaluation of the strength of the conclusion, and hence discusses the relation of the conclusion with the premisses. The possibility of true conclusions following from false premisses is discussed extensively on a syllogistic basis. In addition the circular syllogism and the conversion of syllogisms (by reduction and "per impossibile"), together with induction and deduction, are analysed.

(7) *De categoricis syllogismis*, as yet unedited, is a paraphrase of Boethius' work on the categorical syllogism and deals exclusively with the three figures of this syllogism, neglecting the modal syllogism entirely.

(8) *De hypotheticis syllogismis*, also unedited, paraphrases Boethius' treatise of the hypothetical syllogism. It is concerned with those syllogisms whose major premiss at least is a compound proposition. The conditional and disjunctive syllogisms are discussed, the former *in extenso*. The whole manner of treating these syllogisms indicates that in Boethius we are still confronted with a logic of terms rather than a calculus of propositions. Though Boethius apparently was influenced by the

Stoic development of the conditional syllogism, his treatment of it would seem to argue that he did not realize the true nature of the logic used to develop it. For we find him explaining these syllogisms as variations of the syllogistic inference with its three figures and respective modes, thus reducing the hypothetical syllogism to another instance of the Aristotelian logic of classes having little or nothing in common with the relationship of propositions as such. Rudiments of this tract on the hypothetical syllogism can still be found in neo-scholastic textbooks.

(9) *Posteriora Analytica* (Vol. II, pp. 1-232). In this paraphrase on Aristotle's *Posterior Analytics*, St. Albert has transmitted the Aristotelian theory of demonstration. According to the Stagirite, the demonstrative syllogism is one in which, from necessary and evident premisses, a necessary conclusion is inferred. The theory itself is elaborated in the first book. The second deals chiefly with the problem of definition and its rôle in demonstration. The *Posterior Analytics*, which might well be called "Aristotelian axiomatics", indicates how completely Aristotle was guided by the mathematical ideal. His idea of a demonstrative science has deeply influenced the scholastic discussions on the nature and properties of a true science. It would seem, however, that this portion of the Aristotelian legacy was transmitted principally through Robert Grosseteste's *Commentary on the Posterior Analytics* rather than that of St. Albert, at least so far as the Oxonian scholasticism is concerned.

(10) *Topica* (Vol. II, pp. 233-524) is concerned with the dialectical rules or "principles"[9] which enable one to arrive at probable solutions to various problems. Historically speaking, we are justified in regarding this rather strange logical work of Aristotle as the starting-point for the medieval theory of the "consequentiae" as well as the tract on the "Obligationes" (Art of disputation); for not only did the *Topics* provide rules for this art, but in their study of the enthymematic character of the inferences employed, the scholastics were gradually led to investigate the interrelationship of proposi-

tions under the broader aspects of extra-syllogistic inferences.

(11) *Elenchi* (Vol. II, pp. 525-713). The last book of the Aristotelian topics was known to the scholastics as a special tract entitled *On Sophistical Refutation* (*De sophisticis elenchis*), comprising two parts or books. In Albert's paraphrase the Scholastics became acquainted with an ingenious tract on fallacies.

This is the legacy of logic definitely at the disposal of the schoolmen around the middle of the 13th century, made palatable through Albert's paraphrase. It may be understood as a type of Aristotelian logic, if we take the term in a broader sense than defined above. It contains certain neo-platonic elements and, as Albert does not hesitate to remind us, many Arabian ingredients also. What is most conspicuous by its absence in this logical encyclopedia is the Stoic logic of propositions. As we pointed out above, even the hypothetical syllogism is treated on a syllogistic basis. Indeed, the syllogism is the core and centre of this entire theory of logic.

Great and extensive as this legacy was, it was not taken over by the scholastics as something to be squandered or hoarded. Rather it was regarded simply as initial capital to be augmented through careful speculation. Far from making the schoolmen rest content with what they possessed, it stimulated them to push forward the frontiers of their science and strike out for new horizons. How much of the initial development of the scholastic's inheritance is to be credited to St. Albert himself is difficult to determine. Further research will be required to define exactly the extent of his personal contribution.

II

NEW ELEMENTS OF SCHOLASTIC LOGIC

Even as Albertus Magnus was composing his vast encyclopedia of logic, or perhaps even earlier, logicians had begun to exploit their legacy. Certain tracts which were to be of the utmost importance to the future of scholastic logic were developed. We shall call these "new elements of logic", not because they were without root or foundation in the tradition, but only because they are new in the sense that certain aspects of logic hitherto insufficiently treated or neglected were discovered to be of such importance that they were elaborated and developed to such an extent as to give rise to a new terminology and to initiate valuable discoveries. We call them "elements", not in the sense that they are wholly irreducible to the logic of the legacy, but merely because they enjoyed a certain autonomy as separate treatises fully on a par in importance with the major works of Albert's encyclopedia. It becomes quite evident, then, that if we wish to become acquainted with the best efforts of the scholastic logicians, we cannot afford to ignore these treatises. On the other hand, it would be a methodical error simply to study these treatises independently of the logical compendiums in which they are to be found, where they act as a ferment transforming the whole into a new synthesis.

In our present enumeration and brief description of these new elements we have tried to call attention to some of the tracts that have come to our knowledge. The following list remains open and is not intended to be exhaustive. Our characterization will be brief at times, either because the matter will be more fully discussed elsewhere or because the content is rather obvious.[10]

6

(1) *Tractatus de syncategorematibus*

It may suffice for the time being to characterize "syn-categorema" as a term which belongs to the formal struc-ture of propositions, be they simple or compound. Such, for instance, are such words as "every", "no", "and", "if-then" and the like. More information regarding the meaning of this term will be given later. For the present we shall con-fine our observations to a few historical remarks.

It seems that the tract on the Syncategoremata com-posed by William Shyreswood is one of the oldest, at least the oldest at present accessible in a modern edition.[11] The MS. Erfurt Amploniana Q 328 ascribes a similar tract to Robert Grosseteste. Another goes back to Petrus Hispanus. During the 14th and 15th centuries the custom of devoting a separate and independent treatment to these logical terms outside the logical compendia gradually dies out. In Ockham's *Summa Logicae,* as well as in the *Perutilis Logica*[12] of Albert of Saxony, the syncategoremata are treated in a special chapter at the beginning. Here the meaning and general characteristics of these terms are touched on, but the peculiarities proper to the particular syncategoremata are discussed on the occasion of their introduction. This latter method is certainly more reasonable. Nevertheless, we refer to this tract as an "element", not merely because it ap-peared independently, but principally because the scholas-tics themselves realized, as will be seen later, that in the formal structure of logic the syncategoremata have a unity all their own.

Another reason why the later scholastics ceased to treat the syncategoremata as a separate tract may be the fact that the individual syncategoremata had to be treated *in extenso* in connection with the treatise on ambiguous pro-positions. Hence the later schoolmen found it impractical to devote a special treatise to these terms, though they re-cognized their theoretical unity. Hence we can add to the syncategorematic treatise the works on Sophismata.

Sophismata were written by many logicians. The sophismata owe their origin partly to the scholastic disputation,
partly to the very real need of clarifying logical difficulties
through the use of concrete examples. Hence "sophisma"
does not necessarily mean sophistical reasoning or a falla-
cious proposition. *On Fallacies* is an entirely different tract,
closely allied to Aristotle's *On Sophistical Refutations*. Sophisma, on the contrary, is usually an ambiguous or faulty
proposition which requires certain distinctions before the
correct logical sense can be obtained and false interpretations rejected. Hence a sophisma may be aptly described
as a proposition which from a logical viewpoint presents
certain difficulties in virtue of its ambiguous or faulty
formulation.[13]

It was only natural that the discussions on the nature
and function of the syncategoremata should play a major
rôle in such discussions. Typical in this regard are the *Sophismata* of Albert of Saxony, a voluminous work containing no less than 250 such problematical propositions. The
opening lines of this work give us an idea of the nature of
such tracts.

> At the request of some students, I shall—God willing
> —compile a few sophismata which owe their difficulty
> to certain syncategoremata. I shall observe the follow-
> ing order: first, I shall deal with those sophismata
> whose difficulty can be traced back to affirmative
> syncategorematic terms; secondly, with those which
> owe their difficulty to such as are negative or which
> include negative terms; thirdly, with those whose diffi-
> culty is to be attributed to modal determinations such
> as "necessary", "possible", etc.; fourthly, with those
> whose difficulty arises from the aforesaid modes· de-
> termining a proposition. . . .[14]

Such sophismata, regarded by certain historians as more
or less ridiculous, present to the discerning reader a wealth of

information about scholastic logic. For this reason we have added a few samples of this type of treatise in the appendix.

Similar tracts on the sophismata were composed by other scholastic logicians, such as William Shyreswood, Siger of Brabant, Siger of Courtrai, Robert Swineshead, Richard Clencton, Buridan, William Heytesbury, Walter Burleigh. The latter also adds sophismata to his tract on the syncategoremata. We wish to make clear, however, that it is not our contention that such tracts on the sophismata were concerned solely with problems arising from the use of syncategorematic terms. Considerably more research is required to clarify this aspect of scholastic logic. But it can be said that, for certain scholastic logicians at least, a very definite connection exists between the two subjects.

In passing, we might mention that certain tracts called *De exponibilibus*, which deal with such expressions as "tantum", "incipit", "desinit", etc., also pertain to the sphere of the syncategoremata.

(2) *Tractatus de proprietatibus terminorum*

For clarity's sake and to avoid adding to the confusion of existing terminology, we have retained the original title *On the Properties of Terms* in preference to *Parva Logicalia*, which is sometimes used.[15] The various short treatises comprised under this heading often appear as distinct and separate entities in many logical compendia, for instance, in those of William Shyreswood, Lambert, Peter of Spain, Burleigh and Albert of Saxony. Sometimes they are knitted into a highly compact treatise as we find at the end of the first part of Ockham's *Summa Logicae*. Sometimes they appear outside such compendia in the form of an independent treatise, either singly or grouped together as a whole. In the *Catalog of the Library of Erfurt* published by Schum, a large number of such tracts are listed as part of the Amploniana collection.

The following list of the subdivisions to be found in the tract on the properties of terms may give those unfamiliar with medieval logic some notion of the variety of topics treated by the logicians of this period. A more detailed exposition will be presented later in connection with the exposition of the theory of supposition in the broader sense of the term.

(a) *Tractatus de suppositionibus.* This tract is taken in contradistinction to those which deal with special kinds of supposition. The use of this term is not always constant. In the rather restricted sense in which we accept it here, supposition is the acceptance of a substantive term for some thing. A substantive term has signification in as far as it is an arbitrary sign instituted or at least employed for the precise purpose of indicating some object (the significate). It assumes supposition at least when it exercises the function of signification, that is, when it actually stands for the significates. Most medieval logicians maintain that this significative function is realized only when the term is actually used in a proposition. Thus in the proposition: "Man is running", the term *man* (not the predicate *running*) has supposition or supposits, since the substantive term *man* is accepted to signify an individual man (the significate).

At any rate, supposition when restricted to substantive terms leaves the question open whether the term supposits for actually existent individuals or for individuals of the past or future or even for those who are in the realm of pure possibility.

(b) *Tractatus de copulatione.* Copulation or "binding" here refers to the fact that adjectives, participles and verbs are united with a substantive term in a proposition. For instance: "Man is *running*", "Man is *white*". From the examples it becomes evident that "copulatio" concerns the significative function of predicates, which, in the medieval sense, is any term in a proposition that is not the subject of that proposition. This is why many logicians have abandoned the distinction between supposition and copulation and have united both tracts under the one heading of supposition. Such is the case with Peter of Spain.[16]

(c) *De relativis.* "Relative" is understood in the sense of a relative pronoun or other similar terms used in language to refer to another term. This tract, then, deals with the significative function of such terms as: *who, this, that, other than, the same as, his, your, mine,* etc. The logicians adopt the distinction employed by the grammarians and speak of relative terms which refer to substances and those which refer to accidents, or they present relative terms of identity or diversity, etc. The main purpose of this tract, then, is to stabilize and fix the supposition of such relative terms and thus clarify the ambiguity so often caused in propositions by dangling pronouns.

(d) *De ampliatione.* "Ampliatio" is the property of a common or universal term of which the personal supposition is extended to signify not only significates or objects of the present, but also of the past or future, or of the realm of possibility. In other words, the number of individuals signified by the term is enlarged or "amplified". The ampliatio has to be expressed by an appropriate term, usually the verb, as, for instance, in the proposition: "Every man will run", the term "man" is extended or, at least, may be extended or amplified so that it not only supposits for the actually existing man, but also supposits for all future men. Similarly in the proposition: "Every man can run", the term "man" may be extended not only to actually existing men, but also to possible men.

(e) *De restrictione.* "Restrictio" is somewhat the reverse of ampliatio, since it means that the supposition of a common term is limited to a restricted number of individuals. Such limitations or restrictions may be affected by various terms and additions to a noun. For example, the adjective "white" restricts the supposition of the term "man" in the proposition: "Every white man is an animal", to the individuals which are white men. Restrictions also result from the use of the past or future tense of verbs or modalities, etc., or of restrictive adverbs.

(f) *De appellatione.* "Appellatio" concerns the supposition of a term as regards existing things only. It is distinct from Supposition because it is only a sub-class of Supposition; it is distinct from Ampliation and Restriction because it can also be of a singular term, and, furthermore, because it is only limited to existing things. For this reason the term "Caesar" (as the name of a Roman man of antiquity), has signification and supposition, but it has no appellation, ampliation or restriction. On the other hand, the term "Truman", signifying the actually living President of the United States, has signification, supposition and appellation, but no ampliation or restriction. There are logicians, however, who take appellation in a different sense. Buridan, for instance, applies appellation to connotative terms such as "white", which signifies and supposits for the thing that is white. But the term "white" has appellation as regards whiteness, for which it does not supposit, and which it does not directly signify. Hence the term "white" both signifies the subject and "calls for" the form.[17]

According to some medieval logicians, a universal affirmative categorical proposition concerning the present is false, if the subject has less than three individuals or "appellata" for which it supposits. Consequently the proposition: "Every man is mortal" would be false if there were only two men existing.[18]

(3) *De insolubili*

Many tracts have been handed down to us from medieval logicians bearing the title: *De insolubili.* The title, however, is misleading, as the authors themselves usually tell us at the outset. For it does not deal with what cannot be solved, but rather with what is hard or difficult to solve. In a strict sense, the tract *De insolubili* deals with certain antinomies, that is, with propositions which falsify themselves because they contain elements or predicates which, for exterior reasons, reflect on the propositions of which they are parts. For instance, let us suppose that Socrates utters only one proposition and nothing else, viz., "What I am saying is false". The term "false", which has no suppositum here other than the proposition which is uttered, and of which it is a part, is said to reflect on itself.

In order to give an idea about the variety of such insolubilia, we here present a few taken from the logic of Albert of Saxony:

"What I am saying is false" (not a literal translation of: Ego dico falsum), provided I do not utter any proposition other than: "What I am saying is false".

"The proposition which I utter is similar to the proposition that Plato utters." It is understood that Plato utters nothing other than a false proposition.

"This proposition is false." Here it is understood that "this" signifies the proposition in which it occurs, viz. "This proposition is false".

Let us assume that Socrates utters the proposition, "What Plato says is false", and Plato utters the proposition, "What Socrates says is true".

Now let us assume that there are only three propositions given, namely, (a) "Man is an ass"; (b) "God does not exist"; and (c) "Every proposition is false".

We shall assume that Socrates says: "What Plato says is false"; Plato says: "What Cicero says is false"; and Cicero says: "What Socrates says is false".

Socrates says: "God exists". Plato says: "Only what Socrates says is true". We further assume that nobody else utters any proposition.

"God exists and some copulative proposition is false."
We assume that no other copulative proposition exists in
the world but the uttered one.

Let us assume that the following proposition is written
on this page: "The king is sitting or some disjunctive proposition written on this page is dubious to Socrates". Let
us further assume that no other proposition is written on
this page, and that Socrates does not know whether the
king is sitting or not sitting, and then let him read the proposition written here.

Many more samples could be given which would show
that these problems were taken seriously by the Scholastic
logicians as they are by Modern logicians.

Here it suffices to add that many tracts on the insolubilia were composed by such men as William Shyreswood,
Bradwardine, Burleigh, Swineshead, William Heytesbury,
Robertus de Flandria, Thomas Manlevelt, Johannes Ale-
mannus, Hollandrinus, Tartaretus and others. They appear
also in the compendia of Logic as, for instance, in Ockham's
Summa Logicae, as well as that of Albertus de Saxonia.

(3a) *De impossibilibus*

The "impossibilia" belong to the insolubilia, if we
broaden the sense to contradictory statements. Tracts on
the impossibilia, likewise, are quite common.[19]

(4) *Tractatus de obligatione*, or *De arte exercitativa.*

The origin of this tract is probably to be found in scholastic exercises in logic, for there seems to be a definite link
between it and the sophismata accompanying the teaching
of logic since the beginning of scholasticism. Within a relatively short time, definite rules were established governing
such disputes. It would, however, be incorrect to see in
these tracts only a collection of rules for such school exercises, since they contain a nucleus of rules for an axiomatic
method, though in a rather crude form. The obligation must

start with propositions, and for these, at least, it is required that there be no contradiction contained. Such a start, which is called the "laying down" of a proposition or the "positio", with all its variations, seems to be the equivalent of the axiom in the modern sense. Modern axiomatics, similarly, requires only consistency for the initial propositions, and the deductions from this. A further peculiarity of these tracts is found in what is referred to as "imposition", which is the use of symbols largely to mark propositions in their entirety or their parts in order to simplify the inferences.

In order that we may demonstrate that consistency is absolutely required, we here present the 7th rule of the *Obligationes* of Albert of Saxony[20]:

> A proposition to which its contradictory opposite follows must not be admitted. For instance, let us assume that it were posited to you: "A is everything that is not A", you would not have to admit it, for, if this were admitted, you would be forced to concede: "If A were A, A would not be A", and vice versa, because this follows from the position (the *positum*). For, if A is everything that is not A, then, if A is A, A is not A, and, if A is not A, then A is A, since A is everything that is not A.

More details of this interesting tract must be postponed for a special investigation. At this time it suffices to add only that many tracts *De obligatione* are handed down to us. William Shyreswood wrote one (MS. Paris, Bibl. Nat. 16617), and it would seem that even the rules differed according to universities. The Library in Erfurt preserves a manuscript (Ampl. Q. 332): *Tractatus de Obligationibus Cantabrigensem sequens doctrinam.*

(5) *Tractatus de consequentiis*

This is, perhaps, the most important new element of scholastic logic, for it deals with inferences from one simple

C

or compound proposition to another simple or compound proposition. In a later section we shall explain how the theory of consequences comes closest to modern logic.

As far as we are able to judge at the present time, these five tracts can safely be called the new elements of scholastic logic in the sense that has been explained previously. However, we did not, nor do we now, maintain that these are the only contributions of scholasticism to logic. On the contrary, there is a great deal of evidence that many parts of the Legacy, notably the theory of modal prepositions, have undergone a tremendous development at the hands of scholastic logicians.

Although we have called these five tracts "new elements of scholastic logic", it is probable that the scholastics themselves would have rejected this qualification. The schoolmen of the Middle Ages were too deeply convinced that they were the perpetuators of a long-standing tradition in which they lived and which they consciously kept alive. This statement applies to logic too, for, to the best of our knowledge, there has never been anyone who has maintained that there is any sort of opposition between these new elements and the Aristotelian logic, known as the *Ars vetus* and the *Ars nova*. In their opinion, Aristotle had invented logic as a science in its basic form, and posterity had only to continue, to develop and to carry to completion what he had founded.

In testimony of this quite general conviction of the scholastics, we cite an interesting passage found at the beginning of an anonymous little work probably composed during the 15th century. The work, entitled *Copulata tractatuum parvorum logicalium*, affords a welcome opportunity to summarize our previous exposition. The unknown author asks whether Aristotle has dealt with logic in a sufficient manner, in view of the fact that he did not compose tracts on what we have referred to as the 'new elements'. He answers:

First it is to be stated that he (Aristotle) sufficiently completed Logic inasmuch as the being of Logic is concerned. Nevertheless, a few small tracts can be added which serve for the well-being of Logic itself and for its completion.

Secondly, it must be said that although Aristotle did not invent this Logic which is being treated here in itself and in the proper form of these tracts, he discovered, nevertheless, all these tracts in their principles, for he discovered certain principles from which these tracts are further developed and composed. Therefore, it is said of him that he discovered them in a certain way. From this it follows that the Philosopher is to be thanked more than Peter of Spain, because the former discovered the principles which are difficult to detect.

In this regard it must be understood that the tract on suppositions is derived from the first book of Periher-menias where it is said: "Since some are universals, some are singulars". Particular things, however, have discrete supposition. Furthermore, he divides the universal things because there are some universal things which express their thing in a universal manner, and these supposit in a confused manner. There are other things which do not express it universally, and these supposit determinately.

The tract of the *Ampliationes* is derived from the third mode of the fallacy of equivocation, because there it is said that argument from a more amplified term to a less amplified one, or vice versa, is not allowed. He gives an example of this: Whoever was healed is healthy; he who is sick was healed. Therefore, he who is sick is healthy. Here the term "he who is sick" is amplified.

The tract on *Appellatio* is derived from the third property of substance where it is said that the second substance seems to signify this something under the figure of appellation, that is, under the similitude of appellation, because the first and the second substance call for the same and, consequently, seem to signify the same.

The *Obligatio*, however, is derived from the first book of the Prior Analytics and from the ninth book of the Metaphysics where it is said that if something possible is posited to be, nothing impossible follows.

The *Insolubilia* are drawn from the fourth book of Metaphysics where Aristotle says: "It happens, therefore, as has been explained, that some propositions destroy themselves". But an insolvable proposition always destroys itself because it implicitly includes two parts of a copulative contradictory proposition, as is, for instance, the insolvable proposition: I am not speaking.

The *Consequentiae* are derived from various passages in Aristotle. First, from the Prior Analytics where, at the end of the first book, Aristotle gives a few rules of consequences ; and, secondly, from the second book of the Topics, where he makes statements about the consequence in itself and in its contrary opposite.

But the tract on *Distributiones* is drawn from the first book of Perihermenias, where it is said that "every" is not a universal but signifies in a universal manner; now, "every" is a distributive sign.

The tract on the *Syncategoremata* is derived from the second book of Perihermenias where Aristotle teaches how to multiply propositions in reference to finite and infinite terms; but the negation is one *syncategorema*.

This crude and partially artificial derivation of the "new elements" of scholastic logic shows, at least, that the author was convinced that he was a good Aristotelian logician. That he felt the need to prove the Aristotelian authenticity of these tracts suggests that there was also a feeling of their differences from Aristotelian logic. We, who are no longer in the living tradition of the scholastics, are at a better position to appreciate how far they have progressed beyond this logic. The "new elements" are, then, a definite contribution of scholasticism to logic as such. This will be shown in what follows, at least for three of these tracts.

PART TWO

IMPORTANT CONTRIBUTIONS
OF SCHOLASTIC LOGIC

I N THE preceding part we have confined ourselves to a
rather summary survey of the old and new elements of
scholastic logic. It is needless to emphasize the fact that not
all of them are of equal importance in regard to the development of logic. Some of them, however, have been a decisive
factor in developing the high degree of formality which
scholastic logic finally reached. Having selected a few of
these tracts for a closer scrutiny, we find that they contain
the best that scholastic logic has produced, and according
to which its value should be estimated. At any rate, we
consider formalism a positive criterion for such an evaluation.

I

THE SYNCATEGOREMATA AS LOGICAL
CONSTANTS

We have already mentioned in our general survey that
quite a number of tracts on the syncategoremata were
written in the Middle Ages. This fact, and their appearance
as special tracts or chapters in the scholastic compendia of
logic, proves that the scholastics were not unaware of their
significance. In fact, we intend to show that a careful analysis of such terms is a sure sign of a deeper consciousness
of the formality of logic. The reason for this is that the
term "syncategoremata" refers to certain terms which are

necessary for logical discourse and without which logic could not start.

Since we are in the dark as to the first independent treatment of these "logical" terms, we shall, for convenience' sake, take for a starting-point the *Syncategoremata* of William Shyreswood.[21] However, we know a little more about the origin of the term "syncategoremata", for there is a strong indication that the term goes back to the Stoics. Priscian informs us that the Dialecticians accepted only two parts of a sentence, namely, the noun and the verb, since, if they are joined, they constitute a complete sentence. They called the other parts of a sentence the "syncategoremata", that is, the co-signifying words.[22] The Dialecticians, however, were not simply logicians, but Stoics as well, as Priscian himself suggests. The identification of the Stoics with the Dialecticians is certainly more in agreement with the ancient usage of the term, at least so far as logic is concerned.[23] To all intents and purposes, therefore, we here have a definite link existing between scholastic and Stoic logic in that they make use of the same term in the same meaning.

The meaning of the term "syncategorema" in scholastic logic can be classified in two ways. Both will serve our purpose equally well, for both reveal the characteristic function of a syncategorema, and both are offered by scholastics. The one presupposes the theory of supposition, while the other refers to the formal character of the science.[24]

As we approach the characterization of a syncategorema from the viewpoint of supposition, we must remember that the scholastics used a definite language, Latin, with its own peculiar grammatical structure. In this language a sentence is formed through the combination of a noun with a verb or its equivalent. Sentences which are either true or false are called propositions. In addition to the noun and the verb, other expressions or words are found in propositions, and further modifications of the noun and verb are also encountered. Some of these modifications of nouns and verbs have no influence on the truth or falsity of the proposition, and as far as logic or philosophy is concerned, they are irrelevant, being of interest only to the grammarian or rhetorician. On the other hand, some have a definite influence on the truth or falsity of a proposition, since, through their addition or omission, a proposition which was true may become false, or vice versa. For example, the addition of the word "no", or the modification of the nominative case into the genitive case, and the like, changes or may change the quality of the proposition. Among the words, or modifications of words, which have such effects on propositions in which they occur are the following, according to Ockham: Nouns, verbs, conjunctions, prepositions and adverbs. He further adds the common accidents of nouns, such as case and number, and finally, the common accidents of verbs, such as mood, person, tense and number.[25]

All these words have a meaning connected with them, since they are spoken signs to which a distinct mental sign or thought corresponds in the understanding. Without further enlarging on the relation between the mental sign or thought and the spoken word, let us simply admit with the Scholastics that our language has spoken or written terms which, through their association with mental terms, have meanings precisely through this association. Thus, for instance, the terms "man", "red", "not", "if-then" and the like have a meaning which can be explained by a definition. However, not all of these terms have an object which is thereby signified. In other words, some of these terms have objects signified by them, and they stand for their objects or significates in the proposition if they function either as subject or predicate of the proposition without entering into any other union with any other term. On the other hand, there are terms which do not have objects signified by them. They lack at least a definite significate, and since they have no definite significate, they cannot be subject or predicate of a proposition if they are not used in combination with another term, whether this term be composed or not, or whether it be a proposition or not. Admittedly, they sometimes do appear as subject in a proposition, as any word might, but then they only represent themselves and should be, according to a device of modern logicians, set off with quotation marks, as, for instance, in this proposition, "*Every* is a syncategorema". It is clear that no object is signified by "Every" in this proposition. However, when the term "Every" is combined with another term which signifies objects, "Every" modifies or determines the other term as regards the number of its significates.

This, then, is the general nature of syncategorematic terms: They are determinations of other terms or propositions, having no signification when taken alone, but exercising their signification only as co-predicates, which is the literal translation of syncategorema. There is, therefore, a dependence of signification and supposition in a syncategorematic term, not, however, a dependence in its meaning, if by "meaning" the sense of a term is understood. Since they depend in their signification upon another term which has signification or signifies by itself, they are, if taken in their (dependent) significative function, incapable of becoming subject or predicate of a proposition.

This distinction is clearly brought out by the scholastics and is particularly emphasized in the following passage from the Logic of Albert of Saxony:

> A categorematic term is a term which, taken in its significative function, can be subject or predicate, or part of the subject or part of the distributed predicate, in a categorematical proposition. "Man", "animal", "stone", for instance, are such terms. They are called categorematic terms because they have a restricted and

fixed signification. A syncategorematic term, on the other hand, is a term which, when taken in its significative function, cannot be subject or predicate, or even part of the subject or part of the distributed predicate, in a categorematical proposition. Such are, for instance, the following terms: "Every", "none", "some", etc., which are called signs either of universality or of particularity. So, too, the negations, as, for instance, the negation "not", the conjunctions, as "and", the disjunctions, as "or", and the exclusive and exceptive prepositions, as, for instance, "except", "only", and the like; all these are also syncategorematic terms.

To further exemplify syncategorematic terms, let us consider the following proposition: "Every man is running". "Man" is the subject. "Every" is neither subject nor predicate, nor is it part of either subject or predicate. Rather, it is a modification of the subject and signifies the manner of supposition in the subject itself. If "every" were part of the subject itself, then the following propositions would not have the same subject: Every man is running, and, Some man is not running. Consequently, these propositions would not be contradictory, which is a gross falsity.

In defining a syncategorematic term, we have designedly inserted the phrase "taken in its significative function" as applying to these terms, for if such terms as "every", "none", etc., are taken materially, they do function as subject or predicates of propositions. For instance, consider these propositions: "Every" is a sign of universality; "And" is a copulative conjunction; "No" is an adverb. In these propositions the aforementioned expressions or terms are not taken in their significative function since they do not act in the capacity for which they were instituted. Thus, in the proposition, "Every" is a sign of universality, "Every" is no more a distributive term than "no" is a negation in the proposition, "No" is an adverb.[26]

By way of summary, then, we might say that the syncategorematic terms have meaning and signification, but their signification is dependent on a categorematic term which is modified or "disposed" by the syncategorematic term. These terms, then, exercise signification only conjointly with a categorematic term. As Albert of Saxony put it[27]: "syncategorematic terms do not signify a thing or an object but the mode of a thing, whether this thing be a subject, a predicate, a proposition, or a number of propositions, and in this sense, these terms have a significabile complexe".[28]

We should like to mention here, without going into further details, that the scholastics have offered a system or a division of the syncategorematic terms accordingly as they are either dispositions or modes of other terms. Burleigh, for instance, distinguishes the following classes: (1) those which are modifications of the subject; (2) those which are modifications of the predicate; (3) modifications of the composition of the subject and a predicate, that is, of one, or even of several, propositions.[29]

From previous explanation, then, it follows that syncategorematic terms are not included in the basic terms of our object language. Rather, they are additions made to the terms of the object language. Yet, they are of such importance that, without them, logical discourse would be impossible. Hence, they are real, logical terms and, though we could dispense with some of them even in logic, many of them are essential.

We now come to our second approach, which is more in line with modern logic. Lacking an adequate symbolism, the scholastics failed to express sufficiently the distinction between the constants and the variables of logical discourse. Nevertheless, the sharp distinction between categorematic and syncategorematic terms can well be considered a substitute for the modern distinction. Medieval texts convince us that this position can be maintained. In fact, when the scholastics spoke of the distinction between material and formal elements of discourse, they came very close to the modern distinction. For, in modern logic, the formal elements of logical expression are the constants, and are symbolized by signs which are not variables. The material elements are represented by variables of individuals, predicates and propositions, etc. Upon close consideration of examples, we see that the variables are equivalent to the material elements which, in turn, are nothing more than categorematic terms. The constants, in like manner, are symbols of the formal elements which are syncategorematic terms.

In order to illustrate and to emphasize just how acutely the scholastics were aware of this distinction, we shall quote at length a passage taken from Albert of Saxony. To be sure, he does not deal with the syncategoremata or the categoremata "ex professo", but only as a means of clarifying the difference between a formal and a material consequence. This corroborates our interpretation nicely. Albert says:

> A formal consequence is that which holds good for every proposition of similar form. For instance: What is B is A; therefore, what is A is B. A material consequence, however, is one which does not hold good for every proposition of similar form; or as it is commonly expressed, where the very same form is retained, such propositions are not equally valid for all terms. For instance: Man is running; therefore, an animal is running. With the following terms, however, the consequence does not hold: Man is running; therefore, wood is running. We speak here of matter and form in the sense that we understand the matter of a proposition or of a consequence to be purely categorematic terms, that is, the subjects and predicates without the addition of the syncategorematic terms by which the former are joined or disjoined or determined to a certain mode of supposition. The rest belongs to the form. Hence, the copula of categorical and of hypothetical propositions is said to belong to the form. So, too, the negations as well as the signs (of quantification),

the order of the aforementioned to each other, and the modes of signification concerning the quantity of a proposition, such as singularity or universality etc. (all these belong to the form). For instance, modal propositions are said to be a form other than that of the propositions of fact because the copula of modal propositions differs from the copula in the proposition of fact (de inesse). Because of negations and of signs (of quantification), affirmative propositions are said to be of a form different than that of a negative proposition. Likewise, the universal propositions are said to be of a form other than that of particular propositions. Because of universality, on the one hand, and distribution, discreteness (singularity) on the other, singular propositions are said to be of a form other than that of indefinite propositions. Due to the difference in order, the following propositions are of different forms: Every man is an animal, and: (An) animal is every man. The same is true of the following consequence: Every B is A; therefore, every A is B; and: Every B is A; therefore, some B is A. Furthermore, because of the relation (of a relative term) the following propositions have a different form: Man is running, and, man is not running; and: Man is running and the same is not running; for, the second is impossible because of its form while the first is not impossible.[30]

The fact that the syncategorematic terms are the real skeleton of logical discourse may also account for the earlier tendency to accord them an independent and separate treatment. However, as the scholastics developed the formal character of logic, it is not surprising that the syncategoremata gradually came to be presented in their proper place in the general scheme.

II

THE THEORY OF SUPPOSITION

In the middle of the 13th century we already encounter tracts on supposition, although this doctrine was known at a much earlier date. Its origins are as yet shrouded in darkness, but we certainly have grounds for assigning an important part in its development to Abelard and the older grammarians, and, most probably, to St. Anselm.[31]

The term "supponere" and its substantive "suppositio" have assumed various and equivocal meanings. In the English language the term "to suppose" almost exclusively conveys the meaning of the act of laying down an opinion, of assuming an hypothesis, of expecting something to be true, etc. Though the same meaning is quite often connected with the words "supponere" and "suppositio" in the language of the scholastics, yet, in their strictly logical use, these words have a more literal meaning. For "sup-pono" etymologically means to put something under something, or to replace, or to substitute. The idea of substitution was enlarged to embrace logical substitution of a sign for that which it signifies. Thus, "to suppose" means that a term replaces or stands for that which it is intended to signify.

We are convinced that the term "suppositio", in this strictly logical meaning, was used already by logicians of the 12th century, since we encounter it in various forms in the works of theologians at the beginning of the 13th century.[32]

In any case, highly developed tracts on supposition are to be found at the middle of the 13th century in the works

of William Shyreswood, Lambert of Auxerre and Peter of
Spain. Since that time, such tracts simply belong to the
deposit of medieval logic, though they are not usually found
in the commentaries on the writings of Aristotle. Even
theologians began to make increasing use of supposition,
as is evidenced in the works of St. Bonaventure and St.
Thomas. Indeed, it was an indispensable tool for ascertaining the exact logical functions of categorematic terms in
propositions. The Aristotelian logical works were not much
help in this regard, since the Stagirite showed little interest
in the semantic problems, and had centred his logic primarily around the analysis of a logic of classes. The doctrine of
supposition, however, had to take into account a theory of
signification (Semantics), and was forced by its very subject matter to break away from a logic of classes in the
direction of a logic of predicates.

Since supposition is principally, though not exclusively,
concerned with the quantity of terms, it deals for the most
part with the extension or range of predicates in reference
to individuals. On this point the theory of supposition is, to
a very large extent, one with the modern theory of quantification. While the theory of signification studies merely the
sign-relation of terms in general, the theory of supposition
studies the signs or terms as predicates in relation to their
subject or subjects. The universal or universalized terms
are not so much considered as classes, the members of which
are characterized by a predicate, but, rather, as predicates,
which, by various linguistic or logical devices, have a definite
relation to the subject or subjects of which they are predicated.

Though we are convinced that the theory of supposition
at root is comparable to the modern theory of supposition
or with the functional calculus of the first order, actual
comparison is made difficult, in view of the fact that modern
logic uses an artificial language, whereas the scholastics

applied their analysis to a "natural" and a spoken language. Medieval logicians were satisfied with a painstaking and sometimes cumbersome clarification and determination of the structures of the Latin language. In particular they busied themselves with ascertaining the meaning and function of those syncategoremata which regulate the range of predication for categorematic terms.

Modern logic, however, has made a decided step forward in assuming only a few constants which serve the purpose of bringing about an extremely simplified language. With these constants, their definitions and the rules governing their use, the scholastic theory of supposition has disappeared. It has vanished, however, at the cost of creating a new terminology foreign to that of any ordinary language. Though the language of logic has gained in clarity and precision, it has not been without a price. Keeping this important difference between the two logics in mind, we shall not be so prone to overlook the basic similarity masked beneath the apparent diversity.

An indication of this similarity is found in the fact that it is sometimes a simple matter to express scholastic rules of suppositions in modern theorems of the functional calculus. This will become more apparent as we proceed in our considerations. For the time being we select but two instances. The one fits perfectly into the pattern of the modern theory of predicates; the other shows divergent interpretations.

A particular, affirmative, categorical proposition about a state of affairs (propositio categorica affirmativa particularis de inesse) is interpreted by the scholastics in exactly the same manner as by modern logicians. Let us consider the following proposition: Some man is mortal. According to the scholastics, this proposition has determinate personal supposition, which means that the proposition is true, if there is at least one subject (or individual), about which it is true to say: This is a man and this man is mortal. Though there may be more, one subject alone suffices to verify the proposition. Hence, the scholastics state that such a particular proposition is equivalent to a disjunction, each member of which consists of a singular proposition containing the subject of its singularized form. Therefore, we obtain the equivalence: "Some man is mortal" is equivalent to "this man is mortal, or, that man is mortal, or, that man is mortal", and so forth for any individual. Modern logic expresses the same relation in the following equivalence:

$$\exists(x)[\text{Man}\ (x) \cdot \text{Mortal}\ (x)] \equiv \langle[\text{Man}\ (x_1) \cdot \text{Mortal}\ (x_1)]\ \text{v}$$
$$[\text{Man}\ (x_2) \cdot \text{Mortal}\ (x_2)]\ \text{v}\ \ldots x_n\rangle$$

It is quite a different matter, however, if we try to compare the scholastic universal affirmative categorical proposition about a fact with that of modern logic. Let us take, for instance, the proposition: Every man is mortal. Modern Logic interprets this sentence by transforming it into a conditional hypothetical proposition or its equivalents in the following symbolization: $(x)\ [\text{Man}\ (x) \supset \text{Mortal}\ (x)]$. We believe that the scholastics knew of this possibility. However, they were aware that this interpretation changes the categorical proposition into an hypothetical one. Furthermore, they admitted the inference "Some man is mortal" from the proposition "Every man is mortal", which inference cannot be made as such from the conditional formulation. The scholastics, then, insisted on the existential import of a categorical, non-modal affirmative, universal proposition about the present. This could be interpreted to mean that they tacitly admitted an axiom to the effect that there is at least one subject (x_1) which satisfies the predicates. As we shall later see, this tacitly admitted axiom proved troublesome to at least one later scholastic logician who made a notable start towards the modern interpretation without, however, completely attaining it. In any case, the insistence on the categorical to the exclusion of the hypothetical nature of such propositions had hindered the development towards the modern interpretation with the result that a complicated interpretation of these universal propositions developed.

In spite of this difference, there is a parallel interpretation as regards the subject of such universal propositions. For the equivalence established by scholastic logicians that "Every man is mortal" is equivalent to "This man is mortal, and that man is mortal, and that man is mortal", and so forth for every man, finds its corresponding counterpart in modern logic in simply singularizing the individual variable. However, we are at a loss in attempting a comparison of the supposition of the predicate with anything modern logic has to offer. For the (later) scholastics would say that the following equivalence holds: "Every man is mortal; therefore, every man is this mortal or that mortal or that mortal" and so forth for every mortal being. In our opinion, this interpretation shows that these scholastics who adopted it did not understand the universal, affirmative proposition in the modern sense; it likewise shows that the idea of classes was not altogether alien to their theory of supposition.

After this short introduction we now have to set about the task of presenting the theory of supposition more in detail and from an historical viewpoint. Since limited space renders the task of tracing the entire history of this theory impossible, we shall consider a few cross-sections showing the stages of development in successive periods. We shall select Peter of Spain's *Summulae Logicales* as a practical starting-point, and the theories of Ockham and Burleigh as representative of further development. The highly formalized theory of Albert of Saxony is presented in the Appendix.

D

1. Peter of Spain

The tracts in Peter of Spain's *Summulae Logicales*, which are of present interest to us, are arranged, according to Grabmann and Bochenski, in the following order: *De suppositionibus, De relativis, De ampliationibus, De appellationibus, De restrictionibus* and *De distributionibus*.[33] However, we can exclude the tracts on relative terms from our study, since the "supposition" of relative terms is reducible to that of the term to which they refer in one way or another according to the respective meaning of the relative terms. The tract on Restrictions also seems to contain the copulatio, since it deals with adjectives (as well as substantives used as adjectives) and verbs in their restrictive function as regards the main subject. Nor does the *Appellatio* require special attention here, since, in Peter's work, it deals only with the restriction of supposition by the verb "is" which signifies the present. The *Ampliatio* can be omitted here, since it will suffice to have indicated its place in the general theory of supposition. The same can be said about the tract *De distributionibus*, which deals with the common distributive supposition, with special regard to the syncategorematic terms "every", "none", etc.

In the interest of clarity, we shall now present Peter's theory of supposition in a schematic form which shows the main divisions and their subdivisions.

I. Discrete supposition (Suppositio discreta). An example of this type is: Socrates is an animal. In general, we can say that discrete supposition is had when the subject of a proposition represents only one individual; hence, the subject of a singular proposition has discrete supposition. In order to symbolize such a proposition we can use either a special symbol for the individual and combine it with a symbol of a predicate, for instance: $f(S)$, or we can make use of specialized variables, for instance: $f(x_1)$. The latter would correspond to the use of the demonstrative pronoun "this", etc.

II. Common supposition (Suppositio communis). "Common" is understood here as opposed to singular and applies, therefore, only to universal terms, as for instance, "man", "animal", etc. All the following divisions take into account only such common terms.

1. Natural supposition (Suppositio naturalis). In order to reach a clear understanding of this supposition, which was dropped by other logicians, we must refer briefly to Peter's theory of signification. He explains: Supposition and signification are different, since signification is effected through imposing a word to signify a thing. Hence, we assign a word, or spoken sign, to an individual or universal thing. Supposition, on the other hand, is the use of a word which signifies something. Signification, therefore, is prior to supposition. Such a word, because of its signification, is naturally capable of suppositing for everything of which it is able to be predicated. This natural capability for supposition, which, of course, goes back to an arbitrary imposition of a word, is called "natural supposition" by Peter of Spain.[34]

Mullally[35] seems to understand "natural supposition" in the sense of mere "predicability", that is, apart from any function of being subject in a proposition, since, according to him, a substantive term possesses natural supposition when it is considered in itself, that is, apart from its function in a proposition. We doubt this interpretation. For Peter says: "Natural supposition is the acceptance of a common term for everything of which it is destined to be predicated, as for instance, 'man' considered in itself (per se sumptus—that is, unspecified and undetermined by a *definite* predicate) has, by its very nature, supposition for all men, who are, have been, and will be". As far as we can determine, Peter does not deny that supposition occurs only in a proposition. Consequently, natural supposition also has reference to a proposition although it is abstracted from any concrete occurrence in a proposition. We almost believe that natural supposition could be compared to the so-called propositional function of modern logic sometimes symbolized as follows: F ( ) or: $f(x)$. We should not, however, overlook the difference between Peter's natural supposition and modern logicians' propositional function, since in the latter the subject is missing, while in the former the predicate is omitted.

2. Accidental supposition. When we do not abstract from the concrete occurrence of a term but consider it in its context, that is, as the term occurs with something adjoined to it (adiunctum), the term stands either for something of the present, past or future. Such supposition is accidental, since the kind of supposition the term has is determined by what happens to be joined to it.[36]

Accidental supposition is subdivided:

(a) Simple supposition (Suppositio simplex). We speak of simple supposition when a common term is accepted or stands for a universal thing signified by it.[37] For instance, when we say: Man is a species, "man" stands for the universal nature which is represented by the term "man", and not for any individual man. Or, as Peter continues: "man" stands for "man" in general (in communi) and for any thing (logically) inferior. This, of course, is a critical point. Many scholastic logicians, and certainly the so-called "Nominalists", will part company with the realists on this point.

(*) Simple supposition of the subject is always had when the subject does not stand for individuals but for some common nature. Instances are: Man is a species; animal is a genus; rational[38] is a difference.

(**) Simple supposition of the predicate is always had in universal affirmative propositions. For instance: Every man is an animal. "Animal", in this instance, has simple supposition, since, according to Peter, "animal" here stands for only the nature of the genus.

He tries to substantiate his assumption by saying that the inference to the logical inferior, namely, to individuals, is false, for it is false to say: Every man is this animal. As we shall see later, this view is not shared by other logicians who, contrary to Peter of Spain, assign personal supposition to the predicate in affirmative, universal propositions. However, they introduce a different consequence. The same is true about the following.

(***) Simple supposition as regards exceptive terms is given, for instance, for "animal" in the following proposition: Every animal except man is irrational. Since the logical descent or inference to the inferiors or individuals is invalid, simple supposition is assigned to the term "animal".

(b) Personal supposition (Suppositio personalis). When a common term is accepted to stand for its logical inferiors, that is, for its supposits, such a term is said to have personal supposition.[39] The theory of personal supposition admits of a direct comparison with the Quantification theory since it studies the relation of a common term to its individuals or subjects. It is subdivided as follows:

(*) Personal and determinate supposition (Suppositio determinata). We speak of determinate supposition when a common term is undetermined by any sign (indefinite term), or, if it be determined, it is determined by a sign of particularity, as in the following instances: Man is running, and: Some man is running, so that the proposition is true for at least one individual. The term "man" supposits, as far as the term is concerned, for any individual man. Since Peter omits them, the interesting inferences which result from this definition will be discussed later.

(**) Personal and confused supposition (Suppositio confusa). This type is distinguished from the former by the fact that the common term is determined by a sign of universality, and, thus, it is taken for each one of the individuals which it signifies.[40] This is further subdivided. However, Peter seems to drop both the subdivisions required by the sign (of universality) or the mode, and those required by the thing; the former characterized by "mobility", the latter by immobility. In any case, "mobility" characterizes the confused and distributive supposition of the subject of universal propositions; for in such a proposition the subject stands for every individual signified by it, and, hence, is "mobilized". The copula "est" and the predicate in such universal affirmative propositions signify, respectively, the "essences" and the natures contained in every individual signified by the subject. However, it seems that Peter prefers to assign simple supposition to the "est" and to the predicate, rather than personal supposition.[41]

Further details of this theory of supposition must be passed over here. Our purpose was only to acquaint the reader with this theory developed about the middle of the 13th century. We do not maintain that this theory is fully mature. On the contrary, it is incomplete. For instance, it does not take negative propositions into account. To a great extent, it lacks formality, since it is not only burdened with metaphysical considerations, but it also does not make advantageous use of inferences or consequences in the characterization of various personal suppositions. However, Peter's theory, for all practical purposes, marks the historical beginning of an enormous development in Logic.

2. WILLIAM OCKHAM (c. 1285–1349)

Our intention is only to show the main variations of the theory of supposition, the milestones, as it were, in its development. It seems appropriate, then, that we immediately proceed to the theory of supposition as presented by the great English logician, William Ockham. Not that we imply that no important contributions had been made to this theory during the fifty odd years intervening between the appearance of Peter of Spain's *Summulae Logicales* and the first traces of Ockham's theory of supposition in his *Commentary on the Sentences*. On the contrary, even in Ockham's writings, there is evidence indicating far-reaching changes which preceded and influenced him. Yet Ockham, though one of the greatest logicians of the Middle Ages, presents the theory of supposition in so thoroughly a formalized manner, that we feel warranted in selecting his theory as typical of the logic of the so-called Nominalists. The best explanation of Ockham's theory of supposition is to be found at the end of the first part of his *Summa Logicae* (written before 1329).

In Ockham's Logic we encounter a theory of supposition which is firmly entrenched in his conceptualism, and consequently free from metaphysical considerations. His theory, however, is not entirely dependent on his conceptualism. This explains why "Realists" could follow Ockham even in the critical points previously mentioned. We shall also see that Ockham introduces a division of supposition into proper and improper.[42] Furthermore, we shall find simplification of the general theory which is effected through the moulding of what were formerly more or less independent tracts into one organic whole. The tracts on restrictions, distributions, appellations and ampliations, and copulations disappear completely from his work. Their specific problems are discussed partly in the theory of suppositions, partly in the second part of his *Summa Logicae*, where he deals with propositions. Finally, the characterization of the various forms of personal supposition is effected by means of consequences (consequentiae).

According to Ockham, supposition is a property of a term, but only when it is used in a proposition. The natural supposition of the older logicians is no longer mentioned by Ockham. Since, according to him, supposition is a function of a term which is either the subject or the predicate in a proposition, he can characterize supposition by the subject or predicate function of the terms. If the suppositing term is the subject, the proposition denotes that the predicate is predicated about this term or about the demonstrative pronoun indicating the same object represented by the subject-term. For instance, let us consider the proposition: Man is an animal. This proposition denotes that at least one man is an animal; for instance, Socrates. Hence, the proposition "Socrates is an animal" is true, so that by pointing at Socrates it is true to say "This is an animal". On this account it is said that "man" in the proposition "Man is an animal" has supposition, for in the proposition it is denoted that the predicate is truly predicated about the subject or its pronoun. The case of the following proposition is somewhat different, although it ultimately comes down to the same thing: "Man" is a noun. Here, too, "man" has supposition since it is denoted that "noun" is truly predicated about the word "man", and we may even point to this written noun ("man") and say, "This is a noun".

If, however, the suppositing term is the predicate, the proposition denotes that the predicate-term, or a substituting pronoun, is truly subjected in regard to the subject. For by this proposition: Socrates is white, it is denoted that Socrates is this white thing or simply, while pointing to the white thing, that Socrates is this.[43]

It immediately becomes clear from what we have discussed that signification and supposition are not the same. We meet this distinction in the following division of supposition according to Ockham:

(A) Improper supposition. This type occurs when a term is used in its improper meaning. Every term has a certain meaning or a certain signification stemming from its original coinage. This is considered to be its proper meaning and the term so used is said to be taken "in virtue of expression" (de virtute sermonis). When, however, a term is not used in its proper meaning but is employed in a metaphorical sense or in some other figure of speech, it is taken in its improper meaning and has improper supposition. The logician should avoid this supposition, and we should be acutely aware in discussion, especially in those involving the quoting of authorities, of the danger which lies in metaphorical expression. We should always try to ascertain the intention of the author of such an expression since, while metaphorical expression may be false "in virtue of expression", it may be true according to the intention of the author.[44]

(B) Proper supposition. This type is divided into personal, simple and material supposition. In order to understand this division, we must keep in mind that Ockham, along with Boethius, distinguishes three modes of existence of a term. First, the term may exist as a mental entity which is a concept or a mental term. This is a natural sign which, without any interference of the will, represents or makes known that which it signifies. Second, it may exist as a spoken term which is a vocal sound arbitrarily instituted to signify the same thing that the mental term signifies. Such an artificial (spoken) term is associated with the mental term by imposition, and, in virtue of this association, a word is said to have secondary signification since it represents or calls to our minds the associated concept. Its primary signification, however, is the same object which is signified by the mental sign. Third, a term may exist as a written term which is similar to the spoken term except that it is written rather than spoken.[45]

While personal supposition is had only when the term, mental, spoken or written, stands for the significates directly signified by it, simple and material supposition is given then, and only then, when a term does not exercise its significative function, or when it does not directly signify its significates. We can now proceed to a more detailed explanation of Ockham's divisions.

(1) For simple supposition two things are required. First, the term in question, be it mental, spoken or written, must not exercise signification or its significative function. In addition, it must stand for or represent the mental term as such. For instance, in the proposition "Man is a species", "man" does not have a significative function, for the significates of "man" are individual men, but it cannot be said of any individual man, "This man is a species". Hence "man", either as a mental term or as a spoken or written term, has no primary significative function. It "simply" represents the concept "man", which indeed is a species, since it is predicable of many individuals. In the case of the spoken or written term, "man" has only secondary representation, since it calls to mind the associated concept. It is to be noted that Ockham's conceptualism does not admit of any "nature" which is intermediary between the individuals and the common concept. For the Realist logicians, it was this "nature" which constituted the significate of a concept in simple supposition.[46]

(2) For material supposition three conditions must be verified. First, the term must not have a significative function. Secondly, it must not represent or signify indirectly and secondarily the mental term or concept. In addition, it must represent the material sound or written word. Instances of this material supposition would be: "man" is a word, "man" is composed of three letters.[47]

(3) Personal supposition is distinct from the others in this: that a term, suppositing personally, exercises its significative function and stands for the significates which it primarily signifies. Every categorematic term is capable of such personal supposition. Ockham adds the cautious remark that it suffices to say that the term occurring in a proposition is denoted to exercise its significative function, though it may happen, as is the case in false or negative propositions, that a term may have no object or significate for which it supposits.[48]
Personal supposition is further subdivided.

(a) Discrete supposition (Suppositio discreta). This type of supposition is understood in the same sense in which it is explained by Peter of Spain. A similar instance is given: "Socrates is running". "Socrates", just as any term denoting an individual, taken in its significative function, has discrete supposition.

(b) Common supposition (Suppositio communis) includes every personal supposition which is not discrete. Ockham distinguishes types of common, personal supposition.

(*) Determinate supposition (Suppositio determinata). Ockham characterizes this type of applying consequences. He labels these applications with the technical term "descensus" (descent), which means that an inference or a descent is made from the higher (the common term) to the lower (terms denoting individuals). Thus, it can be said that determinate supposition of a term is had when the term makes a permissible "descent" from a proposition in which it occurs as a common term to a disjunction of singular propositions in which this term occurs as singularized. Let us take the following instance: "Some man is white". "Man" has determinate supposition since the following "descent" is permissible. Therefore, "This man is white, or that man is white, or . . ." This lends itself quite easily to symbolization. ("M" is the symbol of "man", and "W" is the symbol of "white"):

$$\exists (x)[Mx \cdot W(x)] \supset \langle [M(x_1) \cdot W(x_1)] \text{ v } [M(x_2) \cdot W(x_2)]$$
$$\text{v} \ldots n \rangle$$

It is obvious that the inference is really an equivalence. For that one member be true suffices for the truth of the disjunction. Hence, if any member of the disjunction is true, it follows that there is at least one individual who is a man and who is white. Owing to the fact that one true individual instance is sufficient to determine the veracity of a proposition in which a term with determinate supposition occurs, this type of supposition is called *determinate*. This supposition applies to the subject and the predicate in indefinite and particular affirmative propositions in which both the subject and predicate have personal supposition, also

as regards the subject in negative propositions of this
type.[49]

(**) Confused personal supposition (Suppositio confusa).
Ockham defines this type negatively by saying that it
is every personal, common supposition which is not a
determinate supposition. The positive meaning will
appear in the discussion of the two main divisions,
namely, pure confused common supposition and distributive confused supposition.

(†) Pure confused common supposition (Suppositio confusa tantum). Again, Ockham characterizes this supposition with the help of consequences. In the proposition: "Man is an animal", the predicate is said to
have "pure confused supposition", since it is allowable
to infer to the individual significates of the term
"animal" only, however, by taking the predicate in
disjunction and not by either inferring a disjunctive or
a conjunctive (copulative) proposition. Therefore, the
inference to "Every man is this animal, or Every man
is that animal, or . . .", is a fallacy. Likewise, the inference from "Man is an animal" to "Every man is this
animal and Every man is that animal", etc., is not
permissible. The only valid inference is: "Every man is
an animal; therefore, every man is either this animal
or that animal or that animal or . . .", etc. On the other
hand, it is possible to infer the universal proposition
from any such proposition (if it be true). Take the
following instance: "Every man is this animal, therefore, every man is an animal". Unfortunately, this inference cannot be expressed in Modern Logic which does
not understand such a universal proposition as a categorical proposition. Hence, we prefer to abstain from
a symbolization of this inference, which, when symbolized as a conditional, automatically loses both its
existential import as well as the meaning attached to
it by the scholastics.

Suffice it to add that such a personal, common and
pure confused proposition applies only to the predicate of a categorical universal affirmative proposition.
In this supposition, Ockham goes beyond the older
logicians who assumed simple supposition for such a

predicate, namely, supposition for the "nature" contained in the subject, though it is true that the older logicians realized that the case was different in propositions such as: "Every man is white". It is not clear from Peter's texts whether he applied simple supposition also to this predicate, "white".[50]

(††) Distributive confused common supposition (Suppositio confusa et distributiva). This type of supposition applies to the subject in all universal, affirmative propositions, and also to the predicate in both universal and particular, negative propositions. Again, Ockham characterizes it in terms of inferential operations. For this supposition obtains whenever from the proposition in which a term having distributive, confused, common, personal supposition occurs, it is permitted to descend to propositions connected by the syncategorematic term "and" (therefore, conjunction), in each of which the term under consideration is singularized. This descent is, of course, possible only if the term has more than one suppositum.[51] Otherwise a conjunction could not be former. However, it is possible to infer the original proposition from one proposition containing the singularized term if only one individual exists.

Let us explain this general characterization by way of an instance. "Every man is an animal; therefore: This man is an animal, and that man is an animal, and . . .", etc., for every individual man. It is obvious that the truth of a universal proposition requires the truth of every singular proposition which flows from it.

Ockham subdivides the distributive confused supposition into "mobile" and "immobile". In the case of the "mobile", no exception or immobilization is made, while in the case of the "immobile", certain exceptions are made by which the supposition of the term is immobilized for certain significates. An instance may clarify this situation. When we say: "Every man except Socrates is running", "man" has confused distributive supposition, but it does not supposit in this connection for Socrates, for, in regard to Socrates, the supposition of "man" is immobilized.

Ockham also deals with the supposition of relative terms, and in various parts of his Logic he treats of the supposition of terms in propositions about the past and future, as well as of terms in modal propositions. Terms in certain grammatical structures are also considered. Ockham also formulates rules for them. Since Albert of Saxony decidedly reflects Ockham's influence on him, we prefer to consider these rules in Albert's later and more detailed enumeration rather than here. At any rate, Ockham's work is an important step in the development of the theory of supposition towards a stricter formalization. We notice clearly that Ockham understands supposition as a relation of predicates to individuals or subjects. However, a proposition in ordinary language is usually composed of several predicates. If the general structure of ordinary propositions is to be retained, a complicated interpretation is necessitated. As far as we can determine, this constitutes insurmountable difficulties for the symbolization of such propositions in the language of modern logic. A scholastic universal, affirmative proposition contains much more than a universal, affirmative proposition of modern logic, for it contains existential import.

3. WALTER BURLEIGH (1275–1345?)

From a manuscript preserved in the Amploniana Library in the city of Erfurt, we know that Burleigh wrote his work, *De puritate artis logicae*, after the composition and publication of Ockham's *Summa Logicae*. It seems that he intended his work as a corrective, or, at least, as the voice of a realist in matters of logic, for in 1329 a Friar, John Nicolai of the Danish Province of the Franciscan Order, made an extract or an abbreviation of Burleigh's work, which he prefaces by saying:

> After the aforesaid *Summa* [viz. Ockham's *Summa Logicae*] published by Friar William, Burleigh com-

piled another tract on Logic in which there is really
not much of the useful, since it contains nothing which
is not taken from the preceding *Summa* or from
Boethius' book on the categorical and the hypothetical
syllogism.[52]

This little note, precious for the history of medieval logic,
contains a severe judgment which unfortunately is shared
by several modern historians. Nevertheless, the censure
seems to be too severe and, at any rate, exaggerated. There
is much evidence that Burleigh's sources extend beyond
the limits of Ockham's, Boethius' and even Aristotle's
works. This can be immediately proved from summarily
studying his theory of supposition. Burleigh was not inspired solely by Ockham, for Peter of Spain and other
older logicians of the realistic school also certainly influenced his tract. Despite his dependence on sources, which
is the case with all scholastics, there is evidence that Burleigh surpassed his realistic ancestors in many respects.

At the very beginning[53] of his tract on supposition,
Burleigh makes it clear that properties of terms, other than
signification, belong to terms only as they are found in
propositions. Of the many properties previously discussed,
he treats only of supposition, appellation and copulation.
He defines or determines them as follows: Supposition is
a property of the subject in a proposition; appellation is a
property of the predicate in a proposition; copulation is a
property of the verb in a proposition. By verb he understands the verb "to be" and its present, past and future
forms. However, we shall confine ourselves to a treatment
of supposition, since the chapter on appellation and copulation does not offer substantially new information as regards
the functions of terms in propositions.

Burleigh is aware of the fact that supposition can be taken
in a broad sense and in a strict sense. Taken in its broader
sense, supposition comprehends appellation and copulation

as well. In the strict sense, it concerns only the property of the subject as related to a predicate in a proposition.[54]

Supposition, taken in this strict sense, is divided into various forms, each of which has a different value.[55] The main division is the same as proposed by Ockham, namely, proper and improper supposition. Burleigh understands the improper supposition in the same sense as does the "Venerabilis Inceptor". Even the formula "de virtute sermonis" —in virtue of the expression—occurs frequently, and this formula is by no means characteristic of Ockham or the so-called Nominalistic school. Passing over the supposition of metaphorical words, we now proceed to present the subdivisions of proper supposition.

Proper supposition, which is had when a term supposits for that for which, in virtue of the expression, it is allowed to supposit, is subdivided into material and formal supposition. Although this distinction does not date back to Peter of Spain, it does go at least as far back as William Shyreswood. In fact, Peter of Spain does not even mention the material supposition. It is understood by all logicians in the same sense, viz. as the supposition of a material word without any significative function, as in the instance, "Man" is composed of three letters. William Shyreswood defines it as occurring "when the expression itself supposits for the very sound of the word taken absolutely, or for the expression composed of the sound and its signification". The first case is represented in the instance given above. The second case is represented by the following instance, "Man" is a noun. "Man", in this instance, is a significative sound, though it is not taken in its significative function.[56] Burleigh takes material supposition in a similar sense when he states that it occurs when a word-sound supposits for itself or for another word (or other words) which, however, is not subordinated to this word.[57] We can forgo presenting an instance of the first case. The instance of the second case, however, given by Burleigh, takes on a certain interest. We must leave it in Latin, since it is difficult, if not impossible, to adequately render the "accusativus cum infinitivo" in idomatic English. The instance is as follows: "Hominem esse animal, est propositio vera". According to Burleigh, the expression "hominem esse animal" has material supposition, although it supposits not for itself, but for another proposition of which it is only another grammatical form and to which it is not logically subordinated. This other proposition is: "Homo est animal". It is difficult to see the advantage of such a material supposition in which the "accusativus cum infinitivo" takes the place of its corresponding proposition in which the verb is in the indicative mode. Burleigh, in spite of his promise of brevity, adds to material supposition five subdivisions which can be omitted here.

We are primarily interested in his explanation and division of formal supposition. As we have already mentioned, the expression "formal supposition" is not found in Peter of Spain's works but seems to be derived from William Shyreswood, and it apparently is a common possession of the later realistic logicians. The expression is not to be found in the tracts of the so-called Nominalistic school, although it is retained by other scholastic logicians and is still in use among neo-scholastic logicians. Burleigh does not give an explicit definition of formal supposition. However, it is safe to state that, according to him, every proper supposition which is not a material supposition is a formal supposition. Indicating the two main subdivisions, he characterizes formal supposition by saying that it is had either when a term supposits for that which it signifies (the "significatum") or when a term supposits for the individuals which are represented by the term (the "supposita"). The first is called simple supposition; the second personal supposition.

E

In order to understand Burleigh's notion of simple supposition, we must take into account his realism and his
theory of signification which he shared with most scholastics, Scotus and Ockham certainly excluded. According to
Burleigh, a term signifies the universal or the concept of
the mind, wherefore, in general, the universal is the significatum of a spoken or written term. The individuals or the
supposita are not signified by the term, but are only the
objects for which the term supposits without directly signifying them.[58] This theory, of course, has important consequences, as we shall presently see.

Simple supposition is subdivided by Burleigh into two
subdivisions. A first simple supposition is called absolute
supposition. It is had when a term supposits for a universal
in so far as it is in many. An instance will make it clear. In
the proposition: "Man is the most dignified of all creatures",
the term "man" has this simple supposition. It is profitable to offer Burleigh's very own explanation of this example, since in it there is revealed his excessive realism,
which underlies the explanation of simple supposition.
After having reviewed some of Ockham's objections against
this very instance, Burleigh continues:

> It is usually said that this proposition: "Man is the
> most dignified of creatures", is true even in so far as
> the subject has simple absolute supposition. I under-
> stand it in this way: Amongst corruptible creatures,
> man is the most dignified creature. When one says:
> Socrates is a more dignified creature than man in
> common (the universal, "man"), it is usually said that
> this is false. For, though Socrates embraces the perfec-
> tion of "man", nevertheless he does not embrace it
> necessarily, but only contingently, so that, if Socrates
> is destroyed, Socrates is not a man. Thus, it is patent
> that this consequence is not valid: Socrates embraces
> the whole perfection of "man" and even a superadded
> perfection; therefore, Socrates is more perfect than
> human nature. But it ought to be added that Socrates

necessarily embraces the perfection of the human
species or he embraces the perfection of the human
species as part of himself. However, neither one nor
the other proposition is true. Thus, this proposition
can be true: "Man is the most dignified of creatures",
viz. in so far as the subject has simple supposition. . . .
Others, however, who say that there is not real unity
outside the mind, except numerical unity, must maintain that this proposition is false "in virtue of expression": "Man is the most dignified of creatures . . . ".
(As indeed Ockham does.)

The second simple supposition is called compared or relative simple supposition. This type is had when a term
stands for or signifies a universal in so far as it is predicated
of many. The classical example is: "Man is a species". The
term "man" here stands for a universal in so far as it is predicable of or compared with all individuals of the species man.

Personal supposition, then, is distinguished from simple
supposition by the fact that, in personal supposition, a
term stands for the individuals or the supposita which are
represented by a term.[59]

The subdivisions of this personal supposition are those of
Ockham, and the division is made on the basis of consequences. Even the "suppositio confusa tantum" is enumerated under personal supposition, though Burleigh had
previously confined supposition to the subject.

Thus, Burleigh's tract on supposition represents a transi-
tional stage or a sort of crude synthesis between the logic
of the older school and Ockham's new logic. Unfortunately,
it seems that it is this form, though with some strange ad-
mixtures, that has found its way into some of our better
neo-scholastic textbooks on logic. In reading Gredt's treatment of supposition, for instance, we discover a similar
division. Gredt's supposition, however, is not characterized
by consequences, but by the addition of consideration,
which belongs rather to the logic of classes.[60] This certainly

is foreign to the classical form of scholastic supposition, which, as far as we know, never mentions the extension of a term.

We cannot close this chapter on supposition without at least mentioning certain logicians, who tried to empty certain categorical propositions of their existential import. MS. 153 (written in the 15th century) of the Dominican Library at Vienna contains an anonymous tract on supposition with the Incipit: "Ad clariorem circa terminorum suppositiones . . ." . The author follows the division of supposition as found in Ockham and his followers, though there are differences in the individual treatment of the divisions and subdivisions. One very important difference is that the author introduces conditional propositions into the consequents which follow, according to the rules of supposition, from the categorical antecedents. However, he introduces the conditional proposition only as an addition to and not as a substitute for the categorical proposition. The few instances contained in the next paragraph might illustrate this point.

Determinate supposition is characterized as follows: Determinate supposition obtains when from a common term having a significative function it is permitted to infer a disjunctive proposition in which every part contains a conditional proposition added to the respective term. For instance: "Man is an animal, therefore this man, if he exists, is an animal; or that man, if he exists, is an animal; or . . .", etc. The addition of a conditional proposition is not required, according to the author, when the proposition is negative.

The pure confused supposition is similarly characterized. An instance will clarify the meaning: "Every man is an animal, therefore: Every man is this animal, if it exists, or that animal, if it exists, or . . .", and so on for every animal.

The confused and distributive supposition is likewise

enriched by a conditional proposition in the consequence. Using the same instance previously employed, we have: "Every man is an animal, therefore: This man, if he exists, is an animal, and that man, if he exists, is an animal", and so on for every individual.

We do not believe that the solution offered by this anonymous author is very ingenious. However, he certainly made a notable effort to get away from the existential import of the scholastic categorical proposition, or, at least, he was of the opinion that there was a serious problem. Yet, his solution only adds complications to the already involved scholastic theory of supposition, even in the much more simplified form as presented by Ockham. This is another reason which shows how necessary it was for an exact logic to abandon the grammar of any "natural" language and to build up its own language.

III

THE THEORY OF CONSEQUENCES

In our consideration of the theory of consequences we approach that field in which we discover some of the finest achievements of scholastic logic. It is in the logic of consequences that the scholastics have reached a high degree of formality, which, in the Aristotelian tradition at least, connotes a high degree of perfection. However, we cannot ascribe complete originality in these matters to scholastic logicians, although we can credit them with the discovery, or perhaps the rediscovery, of many theorems which hold places of honour even in modern logic.

Just as we are in the dark about the origin of the other new elements of scholastic logic, so, too, we lack definite information as to the beginnings of the tract on consequences. To be sure, consequences, or consequential rules, were already known to the scholastics and even to the theologians of the 13th century. Very few of the most basic rules are to be found in the works of Aristotle, and we do not find a theory of consequences of any mentionable size in the *Organon*. Nor can Boethius' work on hypothetical syllogisms be considered as a major source for this tract.

It seems that the theory of consequences developed gradually as the outcome of discussions on and systematizations of the *Topics* of Aristotle: Boethius' *De syllogismis hypotheticis* may have given an additional impetus. The topical rules are presented by Aristotle in the form of enthymemata, i.e. the inference from one proposition to another. However, as true enthymemata, they tacitly presupposed a third proposition which transformed them into correct syllogisms. As we shall soon see, this particular viewpoint of enthymemata served as a basis for the division of the consequences, viz. they are divided according as they require a third proposition or not. This fact lends itself to the reasonable assumption that the topical rules are the historical starting-points of the consequential rules. This is confirmed by another historical fact, namely, the inclusion of non-enthymematic consequences in the discussions which are concerned with or equivalent to Aristotle's *Topics*.

Hence, we believe that the occasional remarks of Aristotle in other works cannot be considered the historical starting-point of consequential rules, since these remarks have led only to a clearer understanding of topical rules and of the division of conditional inferences into those that are enthymemata and those that are not. Thus, out of the *Topics*, numerous dialectical rules, considered useful for debates in matters which did not lend themselves to strict demonstrations, certain rules were singled out and refined, and to these others were added. These latter additions were considered to be of such great importance that a special tract was set apart for them. This tract was called the tract on consequences for which definitions, divisions and a large number of rules were formulated and which finally developed into the most basic part of scholastic logic. For the logic of the 14th century can aptly be characterized as a logic of consequences, since the rules of consequence pervade every tract even to such an extent that syllogistics almost disappear.

Despite the valuable work done by Fr. I. M. Bochenski,[61] O.P., Salamucha and Lukasiewicz, we are still unable to write the full history of the theory of consequences. Hence, once more we shall present certain cross-sections of the theory by considering the treatment accorded it by Ockham and Albert of Saxony. We shall discuss the very notion of consequence which they have developed, the division of consequences which they propose, and finally the consequences found in the works of Ockham and Albert of Saxony.

Important though they are, the modal consequences do not enter our discussion. Bochenski rightly maintains that modal consequences, as developed by Aristotle in his *Perihermenias*, had inspired the scholastics in the development of their theory of consequences. Modal consequences, however, are connected with that large and relatively unexplored field of modal logic which requires much more detailed discussion than we can accord it here. Despite this necessary restriction, we shall, nevertheless, not confine ourselves to conditional propositions, but shall take into account the conjunctive and disjunctive propositions as well.

I. WILLIAM OCKHAM

At about 1300, the theory of consequences had already developed a certain definite pattern. Our first example is Ockham's theory, which serves as a practical starting-point.

We do not find a special tract on consequences in Ockham's *Summa Logicae* unless we consider the third main division of the third part of this work to constitute this tract. Indeed, Ockham deals with most of the consequences, their definition and division in this part. However, most of this part is taken up with a treatment of the topical rules. As we have already mentioned, the consequences had started their struggle for independence from their union with dialectical syllogisms, or enthymematic inferences, or that part of medieval logic which corresponds to Aristotle's *Topics*. Ockham is certainly a witness and a contemporary of this origin of consequences. Our task, therefore, will be that of sifting out a theory of consequences which is embodied in this part of Ockham's *Summa Logicae*. This is not a very difficult task, since the general theory and the general rules enjoy a certain independence and distinctness from the other matter contained in this part.

According to Ockham, a consequence is an hypothetical, conditional proposition. That means that a consequence is composed of at least two categorical propositions which are joined by the syncategorematic terms "if-then" or their equivalents. In order that such a conditional proposition or consequence be true, it is not necessary that the antecedent, which precedes logically or factually, be true, nor is it necessary for the truth of the conditional proposition or consequence that the consequent, which follows from the antecedent, be true; both parts may even be impossible. Ockham, however, adds a positive condition, namely, that we speak of a true consequence or conditional proposition only then when the antecedent infers the consequent. Since at this point he does not offer any further information about the meaning of "inference", we shall determine its proper sense in the discussion about the divisions of consequences.[62]

We find Ockham's division of consequences at the beginning of his tract on topical rules. He there explains various divisions, which, however, are not necessarily subordinated. We shall simply follow Ockham's loose arrangement and shall not supply a systematic order, which he wisely omitted.

First distinction: Consequences may be either factual or absolute. A factual consequence (consequentia ut nunc) is valid at one time and may be invalid at another. Thus the consequence, "Every animal is running, therefore Socrates is running", is valid only if Socrates exists, and, therefore, only for the time of Socrates' existence. If Socrates does not exist, the consequent would be false, while the antecedent, according to the hypothesis, could be true.[63]

An absolute consequence (consequentia simplex), on the other hand, is always valid, regardless of the time element.

Consequently, this type of consequence is had when the antecedent can at no time be true without the consequent being true. The following is this type of consequence: "No animal is running, therefore no man is running". If this proposition is formulated it is impossible that the antecedent be true and the consequent be false.[64]

Second distinction: A consequence may be valid in virtue of an intrinsic means or in virtue of an extrinsic means. The term "means" (medium) is equivocal, as our explanation will show. A consequence which is valid in virtue of an intrinsic means (consequentia tenens per medium intrinsecum) is in reality an enthymema. For, the addition of another proposition to the antecedent transforms this consequence into a syllogism. Consequently, intrinsic means could aptly be translated as "premise". Hence, Ockham expressly states that syllogisms are valid in virtue of such "means". For instance: The consequence, "Socrates is not running, therefore a man is not running", is valid in virtue of the proposition, "Socrates is a man", which transforms the consequence into the syllogism: "Socrates is not running, Socrates is a man, therefore, a man is not running".[65]

A consequent follows in virtue of an extrinsic means when it is valid in virtue of a general rule, which does not concern the terms as such but which applies only to the structure of the proposition, in which case the terms become irrelevant. Consequently, the consequence will be valid regardless of the categorematic terms.[66] Means in this case is equivalent to a logical rule. Such a consequence is represented by the following instance: Only man is a donkey, therefore, every donkey is a man. The consequence is valid not because of the terms (the variables), nor because of the truth of an additional proposition formed with the two terms, "man" and "donkey", but simply in virtue of the general rule governing the conversion of exclusive universal and affirmative propositions.

It is interesting to note that Ockham realized that even consequences, which are valid in virtue of an intrinsic rule, are ultimately though insufficiently based on an extrinsic rule or a general rule. The instance that we previously used, namely, "Socrates is not running, therefore, a man is not running", requires not only the additional premise, Socrates is a man, but also the general rule that the consequence from a singular proposition to an indefinite proposition is valid. However, as is obvious in our case, this general rule alone is not sufficient to justify the consequence, since the additional premise: "Socrates is a man", is absolutely required.

The third distinction: A consequence may be formal or material. This is the most important of the divisions introduced by Ockham. Let us first discuss the formal consequence. "Formal" is understood by Ockham in the sense of belonging to the very structure of logical discourse. Hence, a consequence which is labelled as formal must be immediately or mediately governed by a logical rule which is not concerned with the content or the terms, but with the very structure of the propositions. Thus formal consequence comprehends both those consequences which hold in virtue of an extrinsic means as well as those which hold in virtue of an intrinsic means. The latter are mediately valid in virtue of an extrinsic means and they are a formal consequence only in so far as they are thus mediately valid. As regards formal consequence, then, it does not matter whether the respective propositions are true or false, whether they are necessary or impossible; the only matter of concern is that the formal structure guarantee the inference, at least ultimately.[67]

Material consequence, then, is characterized by the fact that it is not valid because of a general rule of which it is an instance, but precisely because of the terms which enter the consequence. Since a formal consequence holds regardless of the truth or falsity of the proposition that entered the consequence, and since the truth and falsity of a proposition is determined by the terms which enter these propositions, a material consequence is only characterized by the truth or falsity of the elementary propositions. Therefore it would seem justifiable that we credit Ockham with the knowledge of material implication in the modern sense. His definition, literally translated, is as follows: "A material consequence exists when it holds precisely because of the terms, and not because of some extrinsic means that precisely regards the general conditions of propositions. Such are the following: If a man is running, then God exists; Man is a donkey, therefore God does not exist."[68] As the instances show, we have here a true material implication, for we can characterize a material implication by saying that it is then given, when we admit that any true proposition is inferred by any proposition, be it true or false. In symbolization[69]:

$$p \supset (q \supset p).$$

And it is also characterized by the other relation that a false proposition infers any proposition. In symbolization:

$$\bar{p} \supset (p \supset q).$$

The two instances of Ockham satisfy these formulae, for, if the proposition "God exists" is true—which is the fact, since it is even necessarily true—then any proposition, whether true or false, infers this true proposition. We may take any proposition at random. In the second case, Ockham takes two propositions which will always be false.

The rest of Ockham's divisions can be omitted here, since they are of no consequence in the following discussions. Rather, they concern various types of inferences on a different level of language and of affirmative and negative propositions. Special names are not even given to them.

We shall now proceed to a survey of consequences

already known by Ockham. In this consideration we shall confine ourselves to those consequences which have corresponding theorems (or theses) of the propositional calculus, since some of the theorems of the functional calculus were explained in connection with the theory of supposition. In this regard, however, we are not aiming at an exhaustive enumeration, since such a step would necessarily lead to a useless repetition if we were to explain in detail all these consequences. Instead of this, we shall follow the method of presenting first the consequential rule in translation, with the Latin text immediately following; secondly, an explanation and instance of the rule, and, finally, the corresponding theorem or thesis of the rule in symbolization.[70]

C 1   From something true, something false never follows. Ex vero numquam sequitur falsum.[71]

Hence, when the antecedent is true and the consequent is false, the consequence is not valid. In fact, this is a sufficient condition for the invalidity of a consequence. Ockham does not give an instance of this rule, for any consequence or conditional inference could serve as an instance. For the symbolization of this rule in the form of a thesis, we must take into account that we presuppose the antecedent to be true and that the rule states that, in this case, the consequent must also be true, if the consequence be valid. Hence, a true consequence infers that the conjunction of the antecedent with the denied consequent be false. This is symbolized as follows:

C 1a $(p \supset q) \supset \overline{(p \cdot \overline{q})}$.

Since Ockham says that the fact that the antecedent is true and the consequent false is a sufficient condition for the falsity of a consequence,[72] the inverse relation holds, which could be symbolized in this fashion:

C 1b $(p \cdot \overline{q}) \supset \overline{(p \supset q)}$.

The rules corresponding to these two theorems are also expressed in the following manner:

> The opposite of the consequent is consistent with the antecedent, therefore the consequence is not valid.
> Oppositum consequentis stat cum antecedente, ergo consequentia non valet.
> The opposite of the consequent is not consistent with the antecedent, therefore the consequence is valid.
> Oppositum consequentis non stat cum antecedente, igitur consequentia est bona.

C 1c $$\overline{p \cdot \overline{q}} \supset (p \supset q).$$

The combination of C 1a with C 1c yields an important equivalence that is used in modern logic for the transformation of a conditional into a conjunction, and vice versa.

C 1d $$p \supset q \equiv \overline{(p \cdot \overline{q})}.$$

We shall here add a consequence which is related to this rule. Discussing the "fallacia consequentiae", Ockham states that whenever there is a case in which the consequent does not follow from the antecedent, the antecedent will follow from the consequent. Hence, every fallacy of the consequent can be transformed into a valid consequence by interchanging the antecedent and the consequent.[73] Hence we obtain the following consequence:

C 1e $$\overline{(p \supset q)} \supset (q \supset p).$$

However, as Lewis-Langford remark, this theorem holds only in material consequence or implication. (Cf. their theorem, 15, 41.)

In his discussion of the general rule: From something true, something false never follows, Ockham also informs us that the antecedent is everything that precedes the conquent, be this a simple proposition or composed of several propositions. For example, the latter case is given in syllogisms. If all the premises of the syllogism are true, the

conclusion or consequent must also be true. However, it
suffices that one of the premisses be false in order for the
conclusion to be possibly false, provided, of course, that
there is a consequence.[74]

C 2   From false propositions a true proposition may follow.
       Ex falsis potest sequi verum.[75]

The apparent modal formation of this rule should not
mislead us, for the modality only serves to emphasize the
fact that from a false proposition both a true and a false
proposition follow. For this reason, we believe that Ockham's rule expresses the same thing that we have formulated as the basis theorems of material implication, viz.

C 2a $p \supset (q \supset p)$.

C 2b $\bar{p} \supset (p \supset q)$.

Ockham, however, insists more on the negative, or, let
us say, destructive character of his rule. Since from a false
proposition a true proposition may follow, the consequence,
"The antecedent is false, therefore the consequent is false",
does not hold. In symbolization:

$$[(p \supset q) \cdot \bar{p}] \supset \bar{q}.$$

On the other hand, the following rule is correct:

    The consequent is false, therefore the antecedent is
    also false.
    Consequens est falsum, ergo et antecedens.[76]

In our opinion, the most natural interpretation of this rule
is to understand it in the sense of the *modus tollendo tollens*
of the so-called conditional syllogism. Consequently, we
offer the following symbolization:

C 2c $[(p \supset q) \cdot \bar{q}] \supset \bar{p}$.

Again, Ockham reminds us that the antecedent is everything that precedes the consequent. Hence, from the falsity
of the consequent, the falsity of the antecedent as a whole

follows, not, however, of a particular proposition, in case there should be more than one proposition in the antecedent. This is especially true in syllogisms referred to by Ockham, though it is also true for any other consequence. Hence we obtain the additional and enlarged consequence[77]:

C 2d $$\langle[(p \cdot q) \supset r] \cdot \bar{r}\rangle \supset \overline{(p \cdot q)}.$$

C 3   In a correct consequence, from the opposite of the consequent the opposite of the whole antecedent follows.

Si aliqua consequentia sit bona, ex opposito consequentis sequitur oppositum totius antecedentis.[78]

This is one of the most basic rules for the logic of consequences, of syllogistics, and the theory of supposition as well. Its most simplified symbolization is this:

C 3a $$(p \supset q) \supset (\bar{q} \supset \bar{p}).$$

Ockham immediately reminds us that the antecedent is everything that precedes the consequent,[79] and, consequently, if the antecedent is a compound (as, for instance, the antecedent of a syllogistic inference), the whole antecedent is false, not necessarily, however, every part of the compound antecedent. This can be symbolized as follows:

C 3b $$[(p \cdot q) \supset r] \supset [\bar{r} \supset (\overline{p \cdot q})].$$

Since it is not specified which proposition is false, we can also symbolize the thesis corresponding to the rule:

C 3c $$[(p \cdot q) \supset r] \supset [\bar{r} \supset (\bar{p} \vee \bar{q})].$$

However, these rules can still be more specified, and that is the main purpose of Ockham's discussion, since he is interested in establishing the rules for the reduction of syllogisms. Though it is not possible to infer from the denial of the consequent (or of the syllogistic conclusion) the denial of one determined part of the antecedent, it is possible, nevertheless, to infer the denial of one determined premise from the denied consequent or conclusion, together with the other undenied premise. Hence we obtain the rule:

> From the opposite of the conclusion and the major, the opposite of the minor premise follows.
>
> From the opposite of the conclusion and the minor, the opposite of the major premise follows.
>
> Ex opposito conclusionis et maiore sequitur oppositum minoris.
>
> Ex opposito conclusionis et minore sequitur oppositum maioris.[80]

C 3d $[(p \cdot q) \supset r] \supset [(\bar{r} \cdot p) \supset \bar{q}]$.

C 3e $[(p \cdot q) \supset r] \supset [(\bar{r} \cdot q) \supset \bar{p}]$.

We know that Ockham presents this rule in a questionable form in his discussion on the reduction of syllogisms (Part III, 1, cap. 11), since he speaks of the opposite of the minor premise which is either the contradictory or the contrary opposite. However, this qualification does not interfere with the two consequences in this case, because he is definitely dealing with contradictory propositions as such. We shall abstain from a discussion of this problem, which is more involved than Salamucha realizes.

C 4   Whatever follows from the consequent also follows from the antecedent.

> Quidquid sequitur ad consequens, sequitur ad antecedens.[81]

C 4a $(p \supset q) \supset [(q \supset r) \supset (p \supset r)]$.

Ockham adds that the rule: "Whatever follows to the antecedent follows to the consequent" is false.[82]

It is noteworthy to mention that Ockham assigns to this rule an important rôle for syllogistics, even for the first figure, and this is also true of the following rule C 5.

In this connection we must add an important rule which is used for the reduction of syllogisms and which Ockham mentions expressly.

F

Whatever follows from the consequent with an additional proposition, follows from the antecedent with the same (added) proposition.

Quidquid sequitur ad consequens cum addita propositione sequitur ad antecedens cum eadem propositione.[83]

The corresponding theorem may be symbolized as follows:

C 4b $\qquad \langle (p \supset q) \cdot [(q \cdot r) \supset s] \rangle \supset [(p \cdot r) \supset s].$

C 5   Whatever precedes the antecedent precedes the consequent.

Quidquid antecedit antecedens, antecedit consequens.[84]

This rule is also important for syllogistics and belongs, as does the preceding, to the so-called principles of the syllogism in modern logic. Ockham further states that this rule follows from the preceding rule, for if Rule C 5 were not true, then it could happen that something follows to the consequent which does not follow from the antecedent. We shall first symbolize the theorem corresponding to the rule, and then briefly discuss Ockham's proof. We offer the following symbolization:

C 5a $\qquad (p \supset q) \supset [(r \supset p) \supset (r \supset q)].$

In his proof, Ockham seems to follow an intuition rather than a strict formal deduction, though, in our opinion, the latter element is not totally absent. Setting aside the deduction of C 5a from C 4a by interchanging the variables and substitution, we may perhaps retrace Ockham's thought in the following manner:

From C 4a follows, by application of the rule, which expresses an equivalence: from the denial of the consequent follows the denial of the antecedent:

$$(p \supset q) \supset [(\overline{p \supset r}) \supset (\overline{q \supset r})].$$

Now, using Ockham's rule in the form of C 1e:

$$(\overline{p \supset q}) \supset (q \supset p),$$

which is also an equivalence, we obtain the theorem C 5a.

However, it is also possible that Ockham followed the opposite line of thought, namely, assuming that the consequent in C 5a is false. This would imply a contradiction with C 4a (as can be shown by retracing the steps of our deduction from C 4a), for, if the consequent in C 5a were false, we would obtain:

$$\overline{(r \supset p) \supset (r \supset q)}.$$

Hence, according to C 1e, it would follow:

$$(r \supset q) \supset (r \supset p).$$

This, however, is a contradiction of C 4a, since, if we were to bring the variables into the same order as in C 4a, we should get the following formulation:

$$(p \supset q) \supset [(\bar{q} \supset r) \supset (\bar{p} \supset r)].$$

This is the equivalent of the other false thesis:

$$(p \supset q) \supset [(r \supset q) \supset (r \supset p)].$$

Or, as Ockham formulates it:

> Whatever precedes the consequent precedes the antecedent.[85]

C 6   Whatever is consistent with the antecedent is consistent with the consequent.

Quidquid stat cum antecedente, stat cum consequente.

We understand the expression "stare cum" in the sense of consistency, or, to be more exact, in the sense that the conjunction of the two propositions is true.[86] Hence the corresponding theorem of this rule can be symbolized as follows:

C 6a $(p \supset q) \supset [(p \cdot r) \supset (q \cdot r)].$

Or:

C 6b $[(p \supset q) \cdot (p \cdot r)] \supset (q \cdot r).$

Ockham again states that this rule can be obtained from the preceding ones. Unfortunately, the "Venerabilis Inceptor" does not make this derivation explicit. He may have Rule C 5 in mind (which in a way is our Rule C 6 in its weaker form), though it is also possible that he has reference to C 3, or the related rule or theorem C 1c. At any rate, the instance he uses shows, at the same time, the fallacy of the invalid rule: Whatever is consistent with the consequent·is consistent with the antecedent. This can easily be shown by instances, since, in the consequence: "Every animal is running, therefore every man is running", the proposition: "Some donkey is not running", is consistent with the consequent. However, it is not consistent with the antecedent, since: "Every animal is running", and, "Some donkey is not running", is a contradiction. Hence the expression:

$$(p \supset q) \supset [(q \cdot r) \supset (p \cdot r)],$$

is wrong, because the consequence of the consequent is not valid. Consequently, the following consequence is valid:

$$(p \supset q) \supset [(\overline{q \cdot r}) \supset (\overline{p \cdot r})].$$

From this we obtain our theorem, by applying the rule C 1c.[87]

C 7   Whatever is repugnant to the consequent is repugnant to the antecedent.
       Quidquid repugnat consequenti repugnat antecedenti.[88]

Ockham explains and proves this consequential rule in a manner similar to the preceding one. The corresponding theorem may then be symbolized either as:

C 7a $$(p \supset q) \supset [(\overline{q \cdot r}) \supset (\overline{p \cdot r})],$$

or as: $$[(p \supset q) \cdot (\overline{q \cdot r})] \supset (\overline{p \cdot r}).$$

Again, the opposite rule (Whatever is repugnant to the antecedent is repugnant to the consequent) is false.

These are some of the general consequences enumerated by Ockham in the special chapter devoted to them. However, there are a few others of equal importance which Ockham explained in an earlier part of the *Summa Logicae*. Since these are indicative of the fact that he had a complete command of the so-called De Morgan Laws, we shall now briefly present them at this point.

A conjunction, or copulative proposition, is a hypothetical proposition formed by the conjunction *and*. For the truth of such a proposition it is required that both parts of the conjunction be true, and for its falsity it suffices that either part of the conjunction be false. This already contains one of the De Morgan Laws, but Ockham does not fail to formulate it expressly:

C 8   The contradictory opposite of a copulative proposition is a disjunctive proposition composed of the contradictory opposites of the parts of the copulative proposition.

Opposita contradictoria copulativae est una disiunctiva composita ex contradictoriis partium copulativae.[89]

The symbolization is obvious:

C 8a $\qquad\qquad (\overline{p \cdot q}) \supset (\bar{p} \vee \bar{q}).$

In this connection Ockham adds a few consequences which likewise belong to the propositional calculus:

There is always a valid consequence from a copulative proposition to either part.

Semper a copulativa ad utramque partem est consequentia bona.

In symbolization[90]:

C 8b $\qquad\qquad (p \cdot q) \supset p$

$\qquad\qquad\qquad (p \cdot q) \supset q.$

Though, according to Ockham, the inference from one part of a copulative proposition to the whole copulative proposition is not valid, it can, nevertheless, be valid because of the matter, that is, if one part of the copulative proposition also infers the other. The invalid proposition would be thus symbolized:

$$p \supset (p \cdot q).$$

The valid consequence can be symbolized as follows:

C 8c $\qquad\qquad [p \cdot (p \supset q)] \supset (p \cdot q).$

As Ockham explains,[91] matter does not derive its meaning from the content of the propositions, but rather from the validity, or the truth of the conditional proposition.

Let us now add a few theorems concerning disjunctive propositions. A disjunctive proposition is a hypothetical proposition which is composed of several propositions connected with the syncategorematic term *or* (vel). In order that such a proposition be true, it is required that at least one part of the disjunction be true.[92]

The corresponding so-called De Morgan Law is formulated as follows:

C 9 The contradictory opposite of a disjunctive proposition is a copulative proposition composed of the contradictory opposites of the parts of the disjunctive proposition.
Opposita contradictoria disiunctivae est una copulativa composita ex contradictoriis partium illius disiunctivae.[93]

The rule is expressed by Ockham in terms of an equivalence, since he states that the same is *required and sufficient* for the truth of the contradictory opposite of a disjunctive proposition as is required and sufficient for the copulative proposition.[94]

Hence we obtain the following equivalence:

C 9a $\qquad\qquad \overline{p \lor q} \equiv (\bar{p} \cdot \bar{q}).$

Again Ockham adds a few rules governing the relations between such propositions:

> From any part of a disjunctive proposition to the whole disjunctive proposition there is a good argument.
>
> Ab altera parte disiunctivae ad totam disiunctivam est bonum argumentum.[95]

He immediately adds, "if no special cause prevents this". It is not altogether clear what he intends by this, but we presume that he has in mind either exponible terms or a disjunction which is denied, a case which is taken into account by Albert of Saxony.[96]

At any rate, we can symbolize this well-known theorem as follows:

C 9b $$p \supset (p \lor q)$$
$$q \supset (p \lor q).$$

The opposite inference is the fallacy of the consequent.

In this connection, Ockham also presents the consequential rule of the disjunctive syllogism:

> From a disjunctive proposition and the negation of one part to the other part there is a good argument.
>
> A disiunctiva cum negatione alterius partis ad alteram partem est bonum argumentum.

For example: "Socrates is a man or Socrates is a donkey, and, Socrates is not a donkey, therefore Socrates is a man".[97] In symbolization:

C 9c $$[(p \lor q) \cdot \bar{p}] \supset q$$
$$[(p \lor q) \cdot \bar{q}] \supset p.$$

In a summary way, these are the propositional consequences which are formulated by Ockham in verbal form and in the form of instances of their respective theses. It has not been our aim to give an exhaustive account of all the rules, but we do hope that we have shown that the scholastics of the beginning of the 14th century were already in possession of a well-developed theory of consequences.

2. ALBERT OF SAXONY

In this section we shall omit the theory of consequences offered by Burleigh and developed by him into an extensive treatment of the hypothetical syllogism in its various forms, for we hope soon to publish his tract *De puritate artis logicae*. An important milestone in the theory of consequences is the *Perutilis Logica* of Albert of Saxony, and we are firmly convinced that it is superior to the *Summa Logicae* of Ockham in many respects. Of course, the great Bishop of Halberstadt was able to profit by the intensive activity in logical research that had been done since the appearance of Ockham's *Summa*. It would seem, moreover, that Buridan has deeply influenced his Logic and it is probable that much of the teaching found in Albert's Logic can be traced back to Buridan.

In Albert's theory of consequence we meet with a careful analysis of the consequential relation. However, we must follow his discussions with the utmost care, paying special attention to the "actus exercitus" and the "actus signatus", or in more modern terminology, we must guard against the confusion arising between *using* a proposition and *speaking about* a proposition.

In his introductory remarks Albert intends to discuss and to explain what is antecedent and what is consequent, what is the sign of a consequence and what are the divisions. After this he presents the various consequential rules.

After the discussion and rejection of various definitions of the meaning of antecedent and consequent, he maintains that the antecedent in a consequence is characterized as follows:

The antecedent is that proposition which precedes another proposition to which it stands in a certain relation. This relation is irrelevant as regards the object signified by the proposition and also as regards the mode of signification. It is required, first, that the same terms be applied in the same meaning, and, secondly, that it is impossible that the antecedent be true without the other proposition being true.

We have presented Albert's definition in a paraphrase which needs some justification, since the text in its Latin form does not readily lend itself to an easy understanding. The text reads as follows:

> Ista propositio dicitur antecedens ad aliam, quae sic se habet ad eam, quod impossibile est qualitercumque est significabile per eam, stante impositione terminorum, sic esse, quin, qualitercumque alia significat, sic sit.[98]

First: To be antecedent to a consequent is a relation of a certain kind. The equivalent of the term "relation" is: "sic se habet ad".

Secondly: The relation regarding truth. The equivalent of "true" is found in the Latin expression: "qualitercumque ... sic esse (or, sic sit)". He defines truth and falsity in this manner: "A true proposition is that which, no matter how, signifies: It is so. A false proposition is that which, no matter how, does not signify: It is so."[99] Hence the definition of antecedent and consequent is based on a relation which regards truth. This relation, however, is strengthened by modal expression.

Thirdly: The impossibility invoked by Albert, when he says that it is impossible that the antecedent be true and the consequent false, does not make the consequence a modal proposition. Therefore, using "I" as symbol of "impossible", we cannot define a consequence by the formula:

$$\text{Def. } p \supset q = I : (p \cdot \bar{q}).$$

The reason is because nothing is said about the modality of
the proposition or even the connection, but something is
said only about the truth-value of such a connection.
Hence, if we admit the modality Verum (V) which Albert,
as Ockham, and, as it seems, most of the scholastics admitted, we could express the relation intended by him in
the following manner:

$$\text{Def. } p \supset q = I : V : (p \cdot \bar{q}).$$

In words: If p is the antecedent to q, then it is impossible
for it to be true that p is true and q is false. We do not think
that we are reading this interpretation into Albert's text,
since he expressly states that the inference from, "It is impossible that it is true that p", to, "It is impossible that p",
is not valid. To illustrate this, let us take the following instance: "If it is true that Socrates is sitting, it is impossible
to be true that Socrates is not sitting". From this, however,
it does not follow that it is impossible that Socrates is not
sitting, since the proposition: "Socrates is sitting", is contingent, and from the contingent proposition follows: It is possible that . . ., and, It is possible that not. . . . Only under
the presupposition that the proposition is true is it impossible that its contradictory opposite be given. Hence the
general conclusion which Albert draws from these and
similar considerations: It is quite a different thing to say:
It is impossible that something is, and, it is impossible to be
true that something is, for something possible can be impossible to be true.[100]

In our opinion, which these instances confirm, Albert defines antecedent as that proposition which is not inferred as
such by the consequent, but the denial of which is inferred
by the denial of the consequent. And that, of course, is
correct.

Having thus determined the meaning of the antecedent
and its corresponding term, consequent, he then briefly

speaks about the sign of a consequence, that is, about the statement connective, *If then* (si), or *therefore* (ergo). By these terms it is designated that the antecedent is antecedent and the consequent consequent.[101]

The consequence itself is a hypothetical proposition composed of an antecedent and a consequent, and a sign or note of consequence, which signifies that the antecedent is antecedent and the consequent consequent. From this definition he infers that there is either a consequence or none. In other words, no consequence is invalid (or, a bad consequence), and every consequence is valid (or, a good consequence). For, if there were a conditional proposition by which it were signified that the antecedent is antecedent, and that the consequent is consequent, and it is so, viz., as it is signified, then there would be a consequence. If, however, it were not so as it is signified, then there is no consequence at all, and consequently, the proposition would be false.

It would seem, therefore, that, for Albert, true conditional proposition and consequence are equivalent.

Similarly, the division of consequences is more systematic than that of Ockham, and is likewise much more simplified.

Albert distinguishes first Formal and Material consequences. We have already explained what he means by *Formal*, namely, everything that belongs to the logical structure of a proposition, and hence only the syncategorematic and not the categorematic terms. Formal consequence, therefore, is that consequence which holds precisely because of the syncategorematic terms contained in the conditional and in its elements.

A Material consequence, on the other hand, is simply true because of the categorematic terms contained in the propositions of the conditional. Since it is not precisely the form of the proposition which accounts for the validity of the consequence, but the material elements of the propositions (the categorematic terms), it would seem to follow that a material consequence is valid because of the truth or falsity of the elements affected by the categorematic terms. This is what is implied by Albert, not only in his description of the material consequences, but also by the subdivision of material consequence. For he explains material consequence as follows: "A material consequence, on the other hand, is said to be that which does not hold for every consequence similar in form, when it is formulated, or, as it is commonly said, which does not hold in any terms, even if a similar form is retained. Take, for instance, this case: A man is running, therefore an animal is running: since it would not be valid if formulated in the following terms: A man is running, therefore a wood is running." This instance should not be misunderstood, for Albert does not deny that the material consequence (i.e., A man is running, therefore an animal is running) can be transformed into a formal consequence. However, the inclusion of animal in man because of the additional proposition: "Every man is an animal", does not interest him here. What is important is only this: Because the proposition: "Man is running", is true, and also the proposition, "Animal is running", is true, there is, therefore, a material consequence.

The subdivision of material consequence implies the same, for material consequence is subdivided into factual consequence, *Consequentia ut nunc*, and into consequence in an unqualified sense, *Consequentia simpliciter*. The material factual consequence is valid only for a certain situation, so that it may be invalid for another situation. He immediately exemplifies it by the famous instance: "Socrates is running, therefore a master of arts is running". The consequence is valid, under the presupposition, that Socrates is *de facto* running, as long as the proposition is true, namely, that Socrates is a master of arts. Here it is that Albert adds that the material consequence can be transformed into a formal consequence if we add the factual truth (Socrates is a master of arts), that is, into the formal consequence of a syllogism.[102]

A material consequence in an unqualified sense, however, which therefore does not only hold in a particular situation, but absolutely, is always valid. But, as has already been excluded, it does not hold precisely because of the form. Consequently, it holds precisely because of the truth or falsity values affected by the terms.[103]

In order to avoid repetition, we shall omit an enumeration and discussion of consequences formulated by Albert of Saxony.

We hope that we have shown that a well-developed theory of consequences was elaborated by the scholastics, that it played a major rôle in their logic, and that they were conscious of this fact. It now remains for us to show that the theory of consequences has decisively influenced the systematization of medieval logic.

PART THREE

SYSTEMS OF SCHOLASTIC LOGIC

THE HEADING for this part of our rather summary inquiry into scholastic logic is not inexact, for there is not only one system of scholastic logic. In the course of medieval history logical knowledge is to be found in many systematizations, which are of interest not only because they are different and varied, but, above all, because they reflect some of the finest achievements of this logic. In our discussion of these systems we shall confine ourselves only to those that are more important. We shall disregard systematizations which are only commentaries on or paraphrases of the "Corpus Logicum", the Ars Vetus plus the Ars Nova.

I. PETER OF SPAIN

The first classical success as regards systematization of logic is undoubtedly that of Peter of Spain. Not that he was the first to essay a system of Logic, but because he achieved such outstanding success that his work became not only a classic but, perhaps, *the* classical work on logic during the Middle Ages. It is preserved in innumerable manuscripts. One hundred and sixty-six editions of his work were made up to the 17th century, when, under the impact of a far inferior logic, the *Summulae* left the classroom.[104]

It is quite understandable that a book so universally distributed—a Greek translation was also made—should undergo some changes at the hands of scribes and printers. Unfortunately, it seems that even in the early manuscripts the original division of the work underwent some change.[105]

As is usually the case with such works, additions were even made in order to meet the teaching needs of the time. Much pioneer work has been done by Grabmann in an effort to determine the original inventory of tracts in the *Summulae*, as well as the order of their arrangements. Bochenski, in his recent edition, has made use of Grabmann's research. We shall, therefore, present Peter of Spain's system of logic in accordance with Bochenski's edition. Since the *Summulae* are a summary of medieval logic as it is found in the beginnings of its great development, we shall add, in parenthesis, the parts of the legacy of scholastic logic corresponding respectively to the parts of Peter's *Summulae*. For clarity's sake, we shall present this schematic view.

   I. Tractatus: *De propositionibus* (corresponding to Aristotle's *Perihermenias*). It deals with propositions in general, starting with a short introduction to Semantics.
  II. Tractatus: *De praedicabilibus* (corresponding to Porphyry's *Isagoge*).
 III. Tractatus: *De praedicamentis* (corresponding to Aristotle's *Categories*).
 IV. Tractatus: *De syllogismis* (corresponding only in part to Aristotle's *Prior Analytics*, since it deals only with the categorical syllogism).
  V. *De locis dialecticis* (corresponding to Aristotle's *Topics*).
 VI. Tractatus: *De suppositionibus*.
VII. *De fallaciis* (corresponding to Aristotle's *De sophisticis elenchis*).
VIII. Tractatus: *De relativis*.
 IX. Tractatus: *De ampliationibus*.
  X. Tractatus: *De restrictionibus*.
 XI. Tractatus: *De distributionibus*.

It is to be noted that the tract *De exponibilibus*, found in the older editions (and also in Mullaly's edition), does not belong to the *Summulae*.

Peculiar and hardly understandable in this arrangement

is the place accorded the *Tractatus de suppositionibus*. We would expect to find it after the tract on *Fallacies*. Its peculiar place here explains the fact that most of the manuscripts and editions have adopted a more logical arrangement. However, Grabmann's evidence in favour of the original arrangement is very strong.

Surprising, though indicative of deep logical insight, is the place assigned to the tract on propositions at the very beginning of this Logic. One explanation for this arrangement could be that Peter needed a short introduction to Semantics and this introduction was provided by Aristotle's *Perihermenias*. In order to preserve the integrity of the teaching contained in this Aristotelian work, he simply continued with it. In any case, the place assigned to the tract on propositions would seem to be typical only of the older Logicans and in those compendia of logic which are contemporary with or directly dependent on the *Summulae*.[106] The systematical significance of the fact that Peter deals with propositions at the very beginning certainly becomes secondary in view of the fact that the tract on Topics or Consequences retains its traditional place after *Syllogistics*.

Finally, a rather peculiar place is assigned the tracts sometimes called *Parva Logicalia*. They are found at the very end of the *Summulae*. Perhaps didactical reasons had induced Peter to effect this arrangement. Perhaps, and we favour this explanation, Peter did not find a convenient place for these tracts in the customary sequence of Aristotelian writings, and, since they really constitute an addition to Aristotelian logic, he added them at the end.

Thus we can say that the first big stride towards a new systematization of logic in the Middle Ages shows serious shortcomings along with some promising features.

2. WILLIAM OCKHAM

We know of two of Ockham's *Summae*: one is concerned with Physics (the *Summulae Physicales*, also called *Philosophia naturalis*) and was only partially completed; the other is his *Summa Logicae*, also referred to at times as the *Summa Totius Logicae*. Both *Summae* are intended as systematizations, using the Aristotelian writings as a basis of their respective branches of knowledge. This accounts for the fact that the sequence to be found in Aristotle's works is the leading principle of systematization. Consequently, we see that the "Venerabilis Inceptor", following the Ars Vetus and the Ars Nova, presents the essence of Aristotelian Logic (including Porphyry's *Isagoge*), adding, however, at appropriate places, the tracts already developed by medieval logicians. Since Aristotelian Logic is centred around syllogistics, the *Summa* as a whole also revolves about this central theme. Ockham deals first with terms, then with propositions, and, finally, with syllogisms. Thus the *Summa Logicae* has three main divisions, each of which has several subdivisions. We shall now present this division.

Division of Ockham's *Summa Logicae*

First Part: *On Terms.*

1. On terms in general (cap. 1-17). It deals with the meaning of the word "term" and its division into categorematic, abstract and concrete, absolute and connotative, terms of first and second imposition, terms of the first and second intentions, univocal and equivocal terms. The problem of universals is also dealt with here.
2. On the five Predicables of Porphyry (cap. 18-25).
3. On the Categories (cap. 26-62 or 63). The first chapters of this subdivision deal with definition and description, the terms "subject", "predicate", "to belong to" or "to inhere in" a subject, and "to signify". Division,

the term "whole" (totum), the meaning of opposition, the term "passio" (necessary predicate), and the terms "being" and "one", all these are also treated in the first chapters. The remaining chapters are devoted to a discussion of the Categories.

4. On supposition (cap. 62 or 63 to 76 or 77).

Second Part: *On Propositions.*

1. On categorical propositions both of fact and modality, including the "exponible" propositions (cap. 1-20).
2. On the conversion of propositions (both "de inesse" and "de modo" propositions) (cap. 21-29).
3. On hypothetical propositions (cap. 30-37).

Third Part: *On Syllogisms.*

I. *On the Syllogism in General.*

1. On the categorical syllogism (cap. 1-19).
2. On the modal syllogism (cap. 20-30).
3. On mixed syllogisms (mixtures of propositions "de inesse" and "de modo") (cap. 31-64).
4. On syllogisms containing exponible propositions (cap. 65-68).

II. *On Demonstration or on the Demonstrative Syllogism.* It contains forty-one chapters of a systematized and developed account of Aristotle's *Posterior Analytics.*

III. *On the Topical Syllogism, or on the Consequences.* This part consists of a thirty-seven chapter, systematized account of Aristotle's *Topics.* The last chapter sets forth general rules for consequences.

IV. *On Obligation,* in seven chapters.

V. *On the "Insolvable" or the Antinomy of the Liar,* in one chapter.

VI. *On Fallacies,* in eighteen chapters.

Abstracting from the tracts which have vanished in modern times, we see that it seems as though Ockham's system of logic is the first to show the arrangement adopted by neo-scholastic textbooks. In fact, Ockham's system is a simple systematization of the Ars Vetus and the Ars Nova adroitly interwoven with the new elements of scholastic logic.

Ockham's logic has certain advantages over the system presented by Peter of Spain. For the first time, as far as we know, the tracts on supposition in general find their natural place at the end of the tracts on terms and before the tracts on propositions, and they are no longer considered as an annex to the traditional Aristotelian logic. Furthermore, the central position of syllogistics in genuine Aristotelian logic is emphasized not only by the place assigned it, but also by the lengthy treatment accorded it, as well as by Ockham's tendency to reduce all inferences to the syllogism, although he is not completely successful in this regard.

Nevertheless, the system of the "Venerabilis Inceptor" has serious shortcomings. The division of logic into three parts, namely, the logic of terms, the logic of propositions and the logic of syllogisms, may be a "natural" one from an extralogical point of view, but it is by no means natural by logical criteria. Other than purely logical, that is, formal, considerations have induced the "Venerabilis Inceptor" to retain the two tracts on terms, despite the fact that he was at least vaguely aware that they were foreign to logic. In this point he simply followed tradition.[107] Furthermore, his tract on propositions is not of such a nature as to form the basis for his syllogistics. This basis must be sought elsewhere.

We now come to the most serious shortcoming in Ockham's systematization. This shortcoming concerns the place assigned to the Consequences. This tract, as we have seen, represents the medieval form of the propositional calculus of modern logic, and as such it has its natural place before syllogistics. To be sure, Ockham had realized syllogistics' dependence on consequences, for in his *Syllogistics* he makes use of consequences and proves certain syllogistic forms with them. At the end of the tract on propositions, he also deals with a few theorems of the theory of propositions. The fact remains, however, that the place assigned to consequences in his logic is among the topical rules, after syllogistics. The only excuse that might be raised for Ockham is that he did not intend a logical system but a "natural" system suggested by the chance arrangement of Aristotelian and other tracts.

3. John Buridan (before 1300–1358)

Though John Buridan's system of logic does not mark a systematical progress as compared with the two systems already mentioned, nevertheless, from an historical viewpoint it is of great interest, for it shows a direct influence of Ockham's system on that of Peter of Spain. Buridan certainly has a place of honour among the logicians of the Middle Ages. We regret that we cannot do him justice, since we have access to only one of his works, *Summulae de dialectica*. This work, however, does not so much mark an original achievement; rather, it is a redaction of Peter of Spain's *Summulae*. However, this rewriting was executed by Buridan, a logician who came from the school of Ockham. Much of the text in Buridan's *Summulae* is the same as is found in Peter's *Summulae*; the arrangement is generally the same, although there are important changes and additions which reveal a great logician. We shall here present this system, and, for the sake of comparison, we shall add the corresponding numbers of the divisions and subdivisions in Peter of Spain's *Summulae Logicales*.

Division of the *Summulae de Dialectica*

I. Tractatus: *De propositionibus* (I).
II. Tractatus: *De praedicabilibus* (II).
III. Tractatus: *De praedicamentis* (III).
IV. Tractatus: *De suppositionibus.*

1. De suppositione in generali (VI and XI).
2. De suppositione relativorum (VIII).
3. De appellationibus.
4. De ampliatione et restrictione (IX and X).

V. Tractatus: *De syllogismis.*

1. De syllogismo categorico (IV).
2. De syllogismo modali.
3. De potestatibus syllogismi.
4. De arte inveniendi (IV).

VI. Tractatus: *De locis dialecticis* (V).
VII. Tractatus: *De fallaciis* (VII).
VIII. Tractatus: *De demonstratione.*

Ockham's influence is immediately apprehensible, for Peter of Spain's *Summulae Logicales* are so arranged by Buridan that syllogistics now occupy a central position, or, at least a position to which the preceding parts lead. Nevertheless, this system too is subject to the same criticisms we made of Ockham's logic. However, we shall soon see that the medieval logicians themselves realized, to a certain extent, the inadequacies of the "natural" system of logic and they consequently arrived at a more logical system.

4. WALTER BURLEIGH

The first scholastic logician who, as far as we know, presented a system of scholastic logic which was quite satisfactory is Walter Burleigh. Despite Michalski's derogatory appreciation of this supposed disciple of Scotus, it seems that Burleigh did not simply fill the world with quite a number of unimportant tracts on logic. We must admit that he had a definite and clear understanding of the formality of logic when he placed the tract on consequences at the beginning of his main work, *De puritate artis logicae.*

Before we go into any further details of this system, a few remarks must be made about the work itself, in which this system is developed. The *De puritate artis logicae* is pre-

served in many manuscripts, three of which are at our disposal. These three are: Erfurt, Amploniana Q 259, Paris,
Bibl. Nat. 16130, Bruges 500. However, the work, as it is
preserved in these manuscripts and in all the others, seems
incomplete. For the work begins with the following lines:
"Suppositis significatis terminorum incomplexorum in hoc
tractatu intendo perscrutari de quibusdam proprietatibus
terminorum quae solum eis competunt secundum quod
sunt partes propositionis. Hunc tractatum divido in tres
partes: Prima est de suppositione, secunda est de appellatione, et tertia est de copulatione."

Anyone acquainted with the medieval custom of intro-
ducing the division of a work will recognize that this division is very inadequate, since it concerns only one particular
tract of the entire work, which contains several other tracts.
Furthermore, something that preceded is presupposed at
the beginning of the tract.

It seems that the beginning of this work, *De puritate artis
logicae*, is preserved in a manuscript at the University of
Los Angeles. The Explicit reads: ". . . quod eodem modo
numeralis ut duo et tria et quatuor possunt categorematice
vel syncategorematice accipi. Et huic operi terminus impo-
natur. Amen. Explicit Burleus minor." The manuscript,
therefore, contains a work of Burleigh and the Incipit
informs us as to which work: "Ut iuvenes in quolibet
problemate disputantes possint esse exercitati et velociter
obviantes quemdam tractatum de puritate artis logicae
propono concedente domino compilare . . .". This work,
therefore, is *De puritate artis logicae*. Yet a comparison
with the other work commonly encountered in manuscripts
shows that the two works are not identical. If we consider
the probability that the work commonly encountered in
manuscripts is incomplete in its beginning (and, as it seems,
also at the end), as well as the fact that the Los Angeles
manuscript contains only a fragment of the intended work,

it seems possible that we have two parts of the one and same work before us. A closer inspection of the two sections yields certain arguments in favour of the assumption that the work in the Los Angeles manuscript is the beginning and the other work the continuation of the *De puritate artis logicae*. Since we are preparing an edition of the entire work where the problem of the unity of the two works will be studied more in detail, it will suffice here to give the division of both works and to show a probable unity in both.

Division of *De puritate artis logicae* of Los Angeles

I. *General Rules.*

1. General rules for consequences.
2. On the nature of syncategorematic terms.
3. On the supposition of terms.

II. *On the Sophistic Art (De arte sophistica).*
III. *On the Art of Obligation (De arte obligatoria).*
IV. *On the Art of Demonstration.*

Of this entire list of matters which are supposed to be treated in the work, only two parts of the first part are actually executed. In other words, the *De puritate artis logicae* of the Los Angeles manuscript ends immediately after the tract on syncategorematic terms. Now it is surprising that the *De puritate artis logicae*, of all the other manuscripts, starts with the third part of the first part of the Los Angeles manuscript, namely, with a tract on supposition containing the introductory phrase: "Presupposing the meaning of terms . . .".

Yet our hypothesis is not without certain difficulties which will reveal themselves in our presentation of the division of the more common work, *De puritate artis logicae*:

I. Tract: *On Properties of Terms in Propositions.*

1. On supposition.
2. On appellation.
3. On copulation.

II. Tract: Without a special heading. In any case, it deals
   with inferential operations which are neither categorical nor modal syllogisms.

      1. On hypothetical conditional propositions.
      2. On hypothetical conditional syllogisms.
      3. On other hypothetical syllogisms.

After the last-mentioned tract there is found in some
manuscripts a tract on *Obligations*, although it has no definitely established connection with the *De puritate artis
logicae*.

It is easily seen that the first tract of this *De puritate
artis logicae* fits into the scheme of the main division offered
by the Los Angeles manuscript. The second tract apparently also fits into the division. However, the first part of
this tract, in part, literally repeats the first part of the
first part in the Los Angeles manuscript. The remainder of
the tract, however, could fit into the general division an-
nounced in the Los Angeles manuscript.

However, a more detailed discussion of this problem is
unnecessary here, since we are mainly interested in the
general division and in certain details found in the MS. at
Los Angeles.

Our first surprise is the complete lack of a special tract
on syllogistics. Neither in the work preserved in the Los
Angeles MS. nor in the other work is there a special tract
which, even in the rudimentary form found in neo-scholastic
logic textbooks, corresponds to the *Prior Analytics* of Aristotle. It is true that the second work contains a long tract
on syllogisms, but, and this is the point, this tract does not
deal with the categorical or modal syllogisms of the *Prior
Analytics*; it deals only with hypothetical syllogisms, that
is, with conditional, copulative, disjunctive and other hypothetical syllogisms. Very little of this discussion is found
in Aristotle's *Prior Analytics*.

We said that there is no special tract on categorical or

modal syllogisms in these tracts. Nevertheless, syllogistics is still there, and this is the second surprise that Burleigh offers. For it is extremely surprising to find that in an "Aristotelian" logic syllogistics are swallowed up, as it were, into another tract which is considered more basic. This tract is the theory of consequences. At the close of his discussion on consequential rules Burleigh adds the following remarks:

> After having spoken about the general rules for every consequence, a few special remarks on syllogistic consequence must be added. I say, therefore, that there are two general rules for every syllogism, no matter in which figure or mode they happen to be, that is, providing that the syllogism has one universal proposition and one affirmative proposition, since nothing follows syllogistically from either a particular or a negative proposition.
>
> Besides these rules common to every figure, there are certain special rules for each figure. In the first figure there are two rules, viz. that in the modes concluding directly the major must be universal and the minor must be affirmative.
>
> In the second figure there are other rules. One of these is that the major must be universal and either one of the propositions must be negative.
>
> In the third figure there are other rules, viz. the minor must always be affirmative and the conclusion particular. If this figure is executed in any other way, the syllogism is invalid.
>
> These remarks about the consequences may suffice.[108]

We thought it necessary to present this entire passage, for this is, in fact, all that can be found on syllogistics in either of Burleigh's two works. To be more precise, this is all that can be found on syllogistics in the first work, since nothing of this nature is to be found in the second, provided, of course, that by syllogistics we mean the theory of the categorical and modal syllogism.

And now the climax. As our scheme of the division of Burleigh's logic demonstrates, the theory of consequences takes its place at the very beginning of a compendium of logic, and the entire logic is built about this tract on consequences. With Burleigh, an historical event of major importance in the history of logic occurred. For the first time in medieval scholasticism—as far as we know—a logician places the tract on consequences, which in turn contains syllogistics as a minor part, at the beginning of his system of logic. The importance of this event is in no way diminished by the fact that later generations have completely forgotten this great achievement. Logic is here conceived in its pure formalism; that is, in its pure nature. We wonder whether Burleigh had this fact in mind when he titled his work *On the Purity of the Art of Logic*. At any rate, the theory of consequences or the theory of inferential operations between propositions is clearly and definitely conceived as the basis and the most important part of logic, not only in theory, but also in practice. What Ockham had merely recognized in theory, without changing the time-honoured position of syllogistics, Burleigh realized *de facto*. At the same time, Burleigh was aware of the minor importance of syllogistics itself. In spite of Prantl's and Michalski's lack of appreciation for this scholastic logician, we feel justified in pleading Burleigh's cause for a position of honour in the history of logic.

5. ALBERT OF SAXONY

Though Burleigh's deep insight into the true nature of logic shared the fate of the first breakdown of scholasticism in the 16th century, it was not forgotten in the 14th century. Albert of Saxony, who is decidedly influenced by Ockham and Buridan, seems to be also under the influence, directly or indirectly, of Burleigh's logic, at least as regards its systematization. Albert's own system of logic, presented in that precious work, which was so rightly called *Perutilis Logica* (a very useful logic), can be aptly characterized as an original combination of the systems of Ockham and Burleigh. In fact, Albert quite often follows Ockham almost literally. Albert often follows him also in the arrangement of the elements of medieval logic. As regards the place assigned to consequences and syllogistics, however, he follows Burleigh. These facts will become evident in the following detailed division of Albert's *Perutilis Logica*, if we compare it with the systems offered by Ockham and Burleigh.

Division of Albert of Saxony's *Perutilis Logica*

I. Tract: *On Terms*.

1. On terms which are verifiable as regards every term.
2. On terms which are verifiable as regards terms of the first intention in material supposition (Porphyry's predicables).
3. On terms which are verifiable as regards demonstrative pronouns designating things, in so far as they are not (language) signs (categories).

II. Tract: *On the Properties of Terms*.

1. On supposition.
2. On ampliation.
3. On appellation.

III. Tract: *On Propositions*.

1. On the various divisions of propositions.
2. On the properties of propositions (conversion, opposition and equivalence). However, the matter is dealt with very briefly and extends into the following tract on consequences (cf. chap. 10).

IV. Tract: *On Consequences*.

1. Discussion of general notions and rules of consequences.

2. Simple consequences (composed of only two sentences).
3. On syllogistic consequences, in general.
4. On hypothetical syllogisms.
5. On modal syllogisms and mixed syllogisms.
6. On topical rules.

V. Tract: *On Fallacies.*

VI. Tract: (1) *On the Insolvable* (one long chapter).
(2) *On Obligation.*

We consider this arrangement superior to that of Ockham, but perhaps inferior to that of Burleigh. However, the *Perutilis Logica* is another important witness for the truly scholastic thesis that the theory of syllogistics presupposes the theory of the consequences and is really only a part of the much more embracing theory of consequences. It is worth while to show that Albert, like Burleigh, is completely conscious of this fact.

The fourth tract deals with the theory of consequences. This is subdivided into several chapters. The first has an introductory character. We made use of it whilst explaining the general idea of consequences and its divisions.

The second chapter deals with material unqualified consequences (consequentiae simpliciter), though some of them, as it is expressly stated, are formal consequences.

The third chapter is devoted to simple formal consequences, that is, with consequences of one categorical proposition of fact (de inesse, not modal) to another proposition of the same kind. We meet here with the elementary theorems of the functional calculus.

The fourth chapter deals with similar consequences but containing terms which are amplified.

The fifth chapter contains similar consequences about the conversion of modal propositions in "sensu diviso".

The sixth chapter deals with the same topic but in "sensu composito".

From chapter three to chapter six, Albert deals with simple consequences, namely, with the consequence from one elementary (in the scholastic sense) proposition to another. Beginning with chapter seven, he starts with formal consequences which are not composed of simple propositions. He says: "After the consideration of simple formal consequences we have now to consider formal syllogistic consequences". There then follows in chapter seven a general discussion of syllogistics in which one term is not in the nominative case. The rest is not of particular interest to us here, and it can be seen in the general scheme of his logic.

From this survey it becomes clear that Albert inserts syllogistics in an organic manner into the system of consequences. The sequence: propositional consequences, consequences of analysed propositions and finally syllogistic consequences is completely in line with modern logic. It becomes clear, furthermore, that in the logic of Albert syllogistics is not only not the central part of logic any more, but has become a subordinated part to the most important part, namely, the theory of consequences. Medieval logic in its stage of maturity in the 14th century has become an essentially consequential logic. A consequential logic, however, is a highly formalistic logic.

Unfortunately, this peak of the development of medieval logic was reached at the beginning of a rapid decline of scholastic philosophy in general. To interpret this chronological coincidence as a causal relation, and to blame the high standard of 14th-century logic for the ruin of scholastic metaphysics, appears to us extremely ironical. We are not convinced that scholastic metaphysics has to be afraid of an inexorable logic. On the contrary, scholastic metaphysics, in contrast with modern metaphysical systems, has called for logical rigour and has always been averse to any kind of intuitionism. We are rather convinced that scholastic logic in the 14th century finally reached a stage by which it was in a condition to justify its basic metaphysical inferences. For it is a fact that the proofs of the existence of God developed during the Middle Ages, and definitely the proofs of St. Thomas, cannot be sufficiently developed and justified with a logic content with syllogistics. This has been shown by Salamucha as regards the first of the five ways of the Common Doctor. It was likewise stated already in the Middle Ages as regards the proof of the existence of God advanced by Scotus. Petrus Thomae, an immediate disciple of the Subtle Doctor, expressly states that consequences holding in virtue of an extrinsic means, and hence not reducible to syllogisms, are used in the construction of his proof.

Historically speaking, then, medieval logic had finally caught up with metaphysics when, for well - known exterior reasons, a general decline of scientific culture began.

CONCLUSION

IT WAS our intention to convey a general idea about genuine scholastic logic. To give a complete picture of its depth and breadth, that is, of its doctrine and historical development, is not only beyond the scope of the present booklet, but for the time being most probably beyond the limits of our ability. The more we have plunged into the immense literature produced in the Middle Ages concerning logic, the more we were reminded of the fact that we are still at the beginning of an almost virgin field which awaits exploration. Our attempt is only one of the very few which can be considered only as a sounding out of the terrain but not as a careful survey of the entire inventory. There is much more in scholastic logic than even our summary treatment might suggest. For instance, we have hardly hinted at the theory of scholastic Axiomatics developed in commentaries on Aristotle's *Posterior Analytics* and in separate tracts on demonstration. We have also kept aloof from the enormous development of the logic of modalities and have barely mentioned the scholastic doctrine on fallacies and antinomies. Yet, we hope that even these few fragments of scholastic logic may give a fair idea of scholastic logic in general. At any rate, they will prove that this logic is very inadequately known at our present time, not to say that it is almost completely unknown to both modern logicians, and, what is even worse, to neo-scholastic logicians; furthermore, that the identification of neo-scholastic logic with scholastic logic is by no means admissible but rather an error caused simply by a similarity of name; finally, that modern logic finds itself more often on common grounds with scholastic logic than with neo-scholastic logic.

If these conclusions are adequately proved and accepted, then we hope they will cause a thorough revision of our neo-scholastic logic. It was this hope that has time and again stimulated our energy. We are witnessing an enormous research activity in the field of ancient scholasticism and a surprising revival of scholastic metaphysics in our times. But scholastic logic, the tool that the masters so ably handled in constructing their systems, is up to now utterly neglected. There is the very acute danger that the scholastic of our day leaves the solid and sound path of his ancestors and indulges in intuition and certain "isms" of which his masters were or would be extremely suspicious.

In order to achieve a neo-scholastic logic worthy of the name, radical changes must be effected in our textbooks, even if our efforts are directed only to a return to the standards of genuine scholastic logic. A simple "representation" of medieval logic can, however, not be our task, lest we scholastics, strong only in the spirit of a school and weak in the spirit of sound progress, would suffer a deficiency which would separate us even more from the masters of ancient times than our own incomplete doctrines in logic. We need the spirit of the great scholastics, the progressive spirit of Aquinas, of Scotus, of Ockham, to mention only a few.

With great satisfaction we have learned of the efforts of certain neo-scholastics—the term neo-scholastic being taken in a very broad sense—to introduce modern logic into neo-scholasticism. What they have done was only partly an innovation, for, in many substantial parts, they have only reintroduced into scholasticism what really belonged to it. If our previous discussions should further encourage these endeavours, this booklet has not been written in vain.

SOPHISMATA OF ALBERT OF SAXONY

O N THE following pages we shall present in translation a few sophismata of Albert of Saxony. The texts are taken from MSS. Paris, Bibliothèque Nationale, f. latin 16134, and Vaticana, Lat. 3057. Both manuscripts are found to contain substantially the same text. We shall add the Latin text only where it is absolutely necessary, though in any case the Latin formation of the sophisma itself will be given. We shall also add comments and especially symbolizations, both, however, in a note section.

10. *Sophisma*

All men are donkeys or men and donkeys are donkeys.
Omnes homines sunt asini vel homines et asini sunt asini.[1]

It is first proved that it is true: For it is a copulative proposition of which both parts are true. This is clear, for one of its parts is this: All men are donkeys or men; this is a true proposition. The second part of it is: Donkeys are donkeys; this is likewise true.[2]

It is argued to the contrary: The sophisma is a disjunctive proposition, of which both parts are false. Therefore, the sophisma is false. The consequence holds. The antecedent is proved: The first part of this disjunctive proposition is: All men are donkeys; this proposition is false. The second part is: Men and donkeys are donkeys; this proposition is likewise false.[3]

Briefly I answer that the difficulty of this sophisma stems not from the fact, as I mentioned before, that a universal affirmative sign[4] is added to a complex term. Nevertheless, I am inserting it here[5] for the sake of this sophisma: All men or donkeys are men, the difficulty of which depends upon that mentioned in the preceding sophisma.[6] The difficulty of the present sophisma, however, originates in the fact that it can be understood either as a copulative proposition or as a disjunctive one. Hence I say: If the sophisma is understood as a copulative proposition, then the sophisma is true, as the first argument proved. If, however, the sophisma is understood as a disjunctive proposition, then it is false, as the second argument proved.

Since, however, in these two arguments that which is required for the truth of a copulative proposition was touched upon, some propositions about them must be laid down which will help us in the following discussions.

The first is this: For the truth of a copulative proposition, the truth of both its parts is required.

This is proved: For, there is a good consequence from a copulative proposition to either of its parts.[7] If, therefore, a copulative proposition could be true, some of its parts being false, then from truth falsity would come. This, however, is manifestly false, for, although from falsity there may follow truth, from truth may not follow falsity.

Second proposition: There is a good consequence from a part of a disjunctive proposition to the whole disjunctive proposition of which it is a part.[8] It follows: You are running, therefore you are running or you are not running.[9] If it does not follow, then concede the opposite of it.[10] Since the consequent is a disjunctive proposition, its contradictory opposite will be a copulative proposition composed of the contradictory parts of this disjunctive proposition.[11] Therefore, the contradictory opposite of the consequent will be: You are not running and you are running. From this, however, in virtue of the first proposition, there follows: You are not running,[12] which contradicts the antecedent, namely, you are running. The consequence, therefore, was good, namely: You are running, therefore you are running or you are not running. The consequence holds in virtue of this rule: Whenever the opposite of the antecedent follows from the opposite of the consequent, the consequence is good.[13]

Third proposition: What has been expressed in the second proposition must be understood only for a part of an affirmative disjunctive proposition, and not for a negative one.[14] This is patent, for it does not follow: You are not running, therefore not, you are running, or you are not running.[15] The reason for this is because with the same right as you would say that this follows, I would say that the following is consequent: You are running and you are not running. Thus, contradictory propositions would follow from the same antecedent. Consequently, these are contradictory propositions: You are running or you are not running, and: Not, you are running, or you are not running.[16] The reason is because the proposition to which a negation is attached is equivalent to a copulative proposition composed of the contradictory parts of this disjunctive proposition.

Fourth proposition: It is sufficient for the truth of a disjunctive proposition that one part be true. This is proved: From one part of a disjunctive proposition to a disjunctive proposition of which it is a part, there is a good consequence, as was stated in the second proposition. If, therefore, the disjunctive proposition were false, yet one part true, something true would infer something false.

From these propositions—together with this: From a disjunctive proposition and the destruction of one part there is a good consequence to the other part[17]—it can be proved that *from something impossible anything follows*.[18] For instance, from this proposition: Socrates exists and Socrates does not exist (anything follows), provided that we also assume this rule: Whenever a consequent follows from some antecedent, then whatever follows from the consequent follows also from the antecedent.[19] It can be argued as follows: From the proposition: Socrates exists and Socrates does not exist, follows something from which it follows that man is a donkey. Therefore, from the proposition that Socrates exists and Socrates does not exist, the proposition follows that Socrates is a donkey. Proof of the assumption[20]: From the proposition: Socrates exists and Socrates does not exist, the proposition follows in virtue of the first (general) proposition: Socrates exists.[21] From this, in virtue of the second (general) proposition,[22] the proposition follows: Socrates exists or man is a donkey. Consequently, the proposition: Socrates is a man or man is a donkey, follows also from this proposition: Socrates exists and Socrates does not exist, in virtue of the rule: When a consequent follows from an antecedent, whatever follows from the consequent, also follows from the antecedent.[23] Furthermore, from this proposition: Socrates exists and Socrates does not exist, it also follows: Socrates does not exist.[24] Behold, therefore, how from this proposition: Socrates exists and Socrates does not exist, it follows: Socrates exists or man is a donkey, and Socrates does not exist.[25] But from this: Socrates exists or man is a donkey, and Socrates does not exist, it follows: Man is a donkey, in virtue of the rule: From a disjunctive proposition and the destruction of one of its parts there is a good consequence to the other part.[26] Therefore, it is proved that from this proposition: Socrates exists and Socrates does not exist, it follows: Man is a donkey. In a similar manner it can be proved in regard to anything impossible.

Fifth proposition: Where one and the same sophisma is a copulative and also a disjunctive one, it is possible that the copulative one is true, of which both parts are false, even though these parts are not the principal ones. This is manifest in our sophisma. If it is taken as a copulative proposition, it is true, but both of its parts are false,[27] though it is true that these parts are not the principal parts of the sophisma inasmuch as the sophisma is a copulative proposition, but inasmuch as it is a disjunctive proposition. However, the principal parts of the sophisma, inasmuch as it is a copulative proposition, are: All men or donkeys are men, and the other would be: Donkeys are donkeys. Both of these are true. Our first proposition has to be understood about such principal parts of a copulative proposition.

Sixth proposition: Where there is one and the same proposition which is a copulative and a disjunctive one, nothing prohibits that both parts of the false disjunctive proposition be true, not, however, the principal parts. This is clear, for the principal parts of our sophisma, inasmuch as it is a copulative one, are true, but not the principal parts of the sophisma, inasmuch as it is a false disjunctive proposition.

72. *Sophisma*

Not something is or you are a man.
Non aliquid est vel tu es homo.[28]

Proof: Of this disjunctive proposition the second part is true, namely, you are a man. Therefore it is true, since, for the truth of a disjunctive proposition it is required that one part be true.[29]

Refutation: Its contradictory opposite is true, namely, this proposition: Something is or you are a man. Therefore the original proposition is false.[30]

Answer: In this sophisma, the denial "not" can refer to the whole proposition that follows it, and then it means that it is not the case that something is or that you are a man,[31] and thus the sophisma is false, or it may refer to *something*, and then the sense is: Nothing is or you are a man, and thus the sophisma is true,[32] as the first argument proved, since the other part of the sophisma is true, namely, you are a man. But then the contradictory opposite of the sophisma is not: Something is or you are a man, but this proposition: Something is and you are not a man.[33] However, this proposition is false, since it is a copulative proposition of which one part is false. This is usually expressed in other words, namely, that in this sophisma there can be a disjunction of the negation or a negation of the disjunction. In the first sense the sophisma is true, because thus the sophisma is one disjunctive proposition in which one negative proposition is in disjunction with an affirmative proposition. In the second sense the sophisma is false, because then the negation is brought over the whole disjunction and it signifies as much as this: It is not the case as this proposition: "Something is or you are a man" signifies. And this is false.

THE RULES OF SUPPOSITION OF
ALBERT OF SAXONY (c. 1316–1390)

ALBERT REPRESENTS Ockham's Logic in a highly developed form. He follows the "Venerabilis Inceptor" in his
general theory, but the distinctive mark of his own theory of
supposition is the elaborate formulation of rules. We shall here
present a substantial part of these rules. Albert's arrangement
will be retained and omission of rules will be indicated. Symbolic formulation will be added where it seems profitable and
appropriate without doing violence to Albert's own conception.
The rules will be numbered as in the original.

I. Rules for Suppositions of Terms in General
(*Perutilis Logica*, tract. 2, cap. 6)

1. The subject in every singular proposition has discrete supposition.
Cuiuslibet propositionis singularis subiectum supponit discrete.

     Instances: Socrates is running; this man is running.

2. The subject of every indefinite proposition has determinate
supposition.
In omni (om. in the ed.) propositione indefinita subiectum
supponit determinate.

     Instances: Man is an animal; man is not an animal.

A remark made by Albert in this context is worthy of special
attention. He admits the view that in material supposition a
term has either discrete or determinate supposition. An instance
will explain what he means. The subject in the proposition:
"Man" is a monosyllable, has material supposition, since it

stands for itself, i.e. for either the sound "man" or the composition of letters made of ink or some other material. Now, "man" in our instance may refer either to itself only, namely, to "man" in the proposition here noted ("man" is a monosyllable), or also to words similar in every respect to this "man". In the latter case, we could say, in a rather awkward manner:

A "man" is a monosyllable (taking for granted, as Albert does, that a particular proposition is equivalent to an indefinite one). Hence, taking the word or sound or written sign "man" as predicate, we can symbolize:

$$\exists(x)\ [\text{"man"}\ (x) \cdot \text{monosyllable}\ (x)].$$

We did not discover any passage in Albert's logic where he admits universal propositions of this kind. However, we found the express admission in a tract on suppositions by an anonymous author of the early 15th century (MS. Vienna, Dominikanerbibliothek 153). Hence he concedes the proposition: Every "man" is a monosyllable. We do not see any reason why Albert should object to this.

3. The subject of every particular proposition has determinate supposition.
   Cuiuslibet propositionis particularis subiectum supponit determinate.

   Instances: Some man is an animal; some man is not an animal.

Albert characterizes determinate supposition in the same manner as does Ockham. Hence the inference to disjunctive propositions containing the singularized subject is allowed: Some man is an animal, therefore this man is an animal, or that man is an animal, or . . . for every individual.

4. Every common term immediately following a universal sign (that is, a sign of universality) which is affirmative and is not preceded by any negation, has confused and distributive supposition.
   Omnis terminus communis sequens signum universale affirmativum immediate sine praepositione negationis supponit confuse et distributive.

   Instance: Every man is running. As we previously explained, such a supposition allows of an inference to a conjunction of an indefinite number of propositions in which the subject is singularized.

Instance of the exception: Not every man is running.

5. A negation makes a common term that immediately or mediately follows it to have confused and distributive supposition.

Negatio terminum communem sequentem se mediate sive immediate confundit confuse et distributive.

Instance: No man is a donkey. In this proposition both the subject and predicate have confused and distributive supposition and the corresponding inferences are valid. Albert, however, adds a restriction to the rule. For the rule holds, provided the predicate is not a singular term and provided no syncategorematic term, added to the predicate, impedes such a proposition.

Instances of the exceptions: Socrates is not Plato. The term "Plato", since it is a singular term, is not capable of common supposition. Socrates is not every man. Though in the proposition, the term "man" has confused and distributive supposition, when it is stated: Socrates is not a man, and likewise though in this proposition, Socrates is every man, again the term "man" has confused and distributive supposition (or, as Albert says, the term "man" is *mobilized* for every suppositum or individual man), the addition of another syncategorematic term, namely, "not", to "every man", *immobilizes* the *mobilized* term "man". That means that in the proposition: Socrates is not every man, the inference to: Socrates is not this man, and Socrates is not that man, is not valid.

Since the case of negative particular propositions is treated by Albert in a special corollary, we shall add it as a rule:

5a. In every negative particular proposition the predicate has confused and distributive supposition, if no other syncategorematic term impedes it.

In omni propositione particulari negativa praedicatum supponit confuse et distributive, nisi aliquod syncategorema impediat.

Instance: Some man is not a donkey. Therefore the following inference is allowed: Some man is not this donkey, and, some man is not that donkey.

Albert mentions that, according to some logicians, the fact
that the predicate in negative particular propositions has confused and distributive supposition is the reason that such propositions cannot be converted by simple conversion. He then
goes on to show the correctness of such a view: For, if simple
conversion of such propositions were allowed, then "animal"
could have determinate supposition in the proposition: Some
animal is not a man, and hence the inference to a disjunction
containing the singularized subject would be valid. But in the
proposition: Some man is not an animal, the same term "animal" would have confused and distributive supposition, and
hence the inference to a conjunction containing the singularized
predicate would be permissible. While the disjunction admits
of false propositions, provided one be true, the conjunction does
not admit of any false propositions, even if one or several
propositions are true. This is the case as regards this conversion.

6. A term made infinite by a negation has confused and distributive supposition.
   Terminus confunditur confuse distributive per negationem
   infinitantem ipsum.

   Instance: A donkey is not-man. It is to be remembered that
an infinite noun is a noun preceded by a hyphen and "not".
Hence the inference is valid to: A donkey is not-Socrates, and a
donkey is not-Plato . . . for every individual man whose name is
predicated together with the hyphen and "not".

7. A relative term expressing diversity causes the term following it to have confused and distributive supposition.
   Relativum diversitatis confundit distributive terminum
   sequentem ipsum.

   Instance: A donkey is different from a man. Since the term
"different" (aliud) includes a negation, namely, "not as", the
predicate is implicitly preceded by a negation, and hence General
Rule 8 follows.

8. A term which includes a negation causes the term following
   it to have confused distributive supposition.
   Terminus includens negationem confundit terminum sequentem se confuse distributive.

This is the same as Rule 7, but expressed in more general terms. Hence a similar instance is given and shall now be explained.

Instance: Socrates is different from a man. Because of the negation included in "different from", the predicate "man" has confused and distributive supposition. If, therefore, the expression "Socrates is different from a man" is correct and true, the following inference to a conjunction containing the singularized predicate must be correct and true also: Socrates is different from this man and Socrates is different from that man, and . . . Socrates is different from the man who is Socrates himself. This, however, is obviously a false consequent, and therefore the antecedent is likewise false. Yet, Albert is willing to admit the proposition if the word order is changed. Here we meet with one of the cases where the highly formalized scholastic logic reveals its subtleties, which we do not consider ridiculous. For that reason we shall explain the different formulation proposed by Albert by applying symbolism.

The relation "different from" contains a negation which can be made explicit by saying: Socrates is not the same as a man. By retaining the apparent particular form of this proposition we can symbolize $(H = \text{Man})$:

$$\overline{\exists(x)}[H(x) \cdot x = \text{Socrates}].$$

This proposition is obviously false. The formulation proposed by Albert places "Socrates" and hence the negation at the end: Socrates ab homine differt. This could be symbolized as follows:

$$\exists(x)[H(x) \cdot \overline{x = \text{Socrates}}].$$

This proposition is, of course, true, since it is true for at least one man who is not the same as Socrates.

We shall here omit the 9th and 10th rules which deal with similar problems concerning the comparisons.

11. Whatever mobilizes an immobilized term, immobilizes a mobilized term.

Quidquid mobilitat immobilitatum, immobilitat mobilitatum.

Instance: Every man is running, and, not every man is running.

In the first proposition the syncategorematic term "every" mobilizes the term "man" for every individual. In the second proposition the syncategorematic term "non", which taken alone has an effect similar to "every", when added to "every" immobilizes the term to determinate supposition. It follows: Not every man is running, therefore at least one man is not running.

II. RULES CONCERNING CONFUSED SUPPOSITION ONLY
(*Loc. cit.* cap. 7)

1. In every universal affirmative proposition the predicate has pure confused supposition, if it is a common term.
   Cuiuslibet propositionis universalis affirmativae cuius praedicatum est terminus communis, praedicatum supponit confuse tantum.

Instance: Every man is an animal. Here "animal" has pure confused supposition and hence the inference is valid: Therefore, every man is either this or that or . . . animal. The printed text adds that according to some logicians the descent is possible not only to the disjunct extreme (predicate in this case), but also to the copulative extreme. This addition, however, is not found in the two manuscripts which are at our disposal.

2. In every exclusive affirmative proposition the subject has only confused supposition.
   Cuiuslibet propositionis exclusivae affirmativae subiectum supponit confuse tantum.

Instance: Only an animal is a man. The reason for this rule is the compound nature of an exclusive proposition which contains several propositions. One of these propositions is: Every man is an animal. In this proposition, "animal" has, according to Rule 1, pure confused supposition, since it is the predicate of a universal affirmative proposition.

3. Every term which is equivalent to an expression composed of a universal sign and a common term causes the common term which follows it and is expressed in the proposition to have only confused supposition.
   Omnis terminus equivalens orationi ex signo universali affirmativo et termino communi, confundit terminum com-

munem expressum in propositione sequentem se confuse tantum.

Instance: There always was a man; there always will be a man. This means that at every time there was or there will be this man, or that man, etc.

4. Certain verbs have the power to cause the terms that follow them to have pure confused supposition.
   Quaedam sunt verba quae habent vim confundendi terminos sequentes se confuse tantum.

Instance: I promise you a dime. "Dime" has pure confused supposition, since I do not promise you a particular dime, but either this one or that one, etc.

III. Rules Concerning the Supposition of Relative Terms
(*Loc. cit.* cap. 8)

1. A categorical affirmative proposition containing a relative term is equivalent to a hypothetical copulative proposition.
   Propositio affirmativa categorica in qua ponitur aliquis terminus relativus aequivalet uni propositioni copulativae hypotheticae.

Instance: Socrates who is running is debating. This proposition is equivalent to: Socrates is running and Socrates is debating.

2. A negative categorical proposition containing a relative term is equivalent to a disjunctive proposition.
   Propositio negativa categorica in qua ponitur aliquis terminus relativus aequivalet uni propositioni disiunctivae.

Instance: Socrates who is running is not debating. This is equivalent to: Socrates is not running or Socrates is not debating.

Albert's proof of this equivalence is developed on the basis of consequences, principally using the so-called De Morgan Laws. Let us symbolize the equivalence by using R for running and D for debating. With a keen insight into the structure of such relative propositions, Albert conceives our particular proposition as a copulative one which is denied. Hence the copulative proposition can be symbolized as follows:

$$\overline{[R(x_1) \cdot D(x_1)]} \equiv \overline{[R(x_1)} \vee \overline{D(x_1)]}.$$

Informal insight confirms this, for, if Socrates, who is running, is not debating, then he may be debating, although it is not a *running* Socrates who is debating. Hence, either part of the copulative proposition which is denied may be false, or, as Albert expresses it: the proposition has two causes of truth, either because Socrates is not running or because Socrates is not debating.

He then adds a few consequences concerning the first and second rules. From the first rule it follows that this is a good consequence: Socrates who is running is debating, therefore Socrates is debating,

$$[R(x_1) \cdot D(x_1)] \supset D(x_1),$$

since, from a copulative proposition to either of its parts there is a good consequence.

From the second rule it follows that this consequence is not valid: Socrates who is running is not debating, therefore Socrates is not debating, because from a disjunctive proposition to one of its parts there is not a good consequence. However, the converse relation holds, and hence the consequence:

$$\overline{D(x_1)} \supset \overline{[R(x_1) \cdot D(x_1)]}$$

is valid.

Of the following seven rules which are given in order to ascertain whether a relative term supposits for the subject or the predicate in the preceding proposition, we shall select only one, the seventh:

> If the antecedent term is a common term, then it is not allowed to replace the relative term of identity by a term similar to the antecedent term.
>
> Si antecedens est terminus communis, non est licitum ponere terminum consimilem loco relativi suo antecedenti.

We must not understand this rule as the denial of a *consequence* which is obviously valid, namely: A man is running and the same is debating, therefore a man is running and a man is debating. For that reason, Albert denies the *equivalence* of the antecedent and the consequence of this consequence. Hence, he continues, it is not the same to say: A man is running and a man is debating, and, a man is running and the same is debating. It is clear that the first conjunction does not infer the second conjunction. Therefore, he admits the consequence:

$$\exists(x)[R(x) \cdot D(x)] \supset [\exists(x)R(x) \cdot \exists(x)D(x)],$$

but he denies the consequence:

$$[\exists(x)R(x) \cdot \exists x D(x)] \supset \exists(x)[R(x) \cdot D(x)].$$

IV. Rules Concerning the Mode of Supposition of Relative Terms

(Loc. cit. cap. 9)

"Mode" here means a kind of supposition.

1. Relative terms of accidents and relative terms of diversity do not have the same supposition as their antecedent terms; their mode of supposition varies rather in accordance with the variation of the syncategorematic terms which are put before them.

   Relativa accidentium et relativa diversitatis non habent eandem suppositionem sicut sua antecedentia, immo variantur modi supponendi secundum variationem syncategorematum eis praepositorum.

   Instance: A crow is black and every Ethiopian is such. "Such" has pure confused supposition, while the antecedent term "black" has determinate supposition.

2. A relative term of identity has the same kind of supposition as its antecedent term, provided it is taken in its relative sense.

   Relativum identitatis supponit eodem modo sicut suum antecedens, et hoc si tenetur relative.

Since the kind of supposition is most easily changed by the addition of a negation, Albert exemplifies the rule by using a negative proposition. Let us assume that Socrates is running and

I

that Plato is not running. This proposition will then be true:
Some man is running and Plato is not that one. (Aliquis homo
currit et Plato non est ille.) The negation preceding the term
"that one" does not change the supposition of it to confused
and distributive, but the supposition remains the determinate
one as in the antecedent term "some man". This he proves by
again applying the De Morgan Laws. The contradictory opposite of the proposition, Some man is running and Plato is not
that one, is: No man is running or Plato is that one. However,
we supposed that Socrates was running (which infers that some
man is running) and that Plato is not running. Hence both
parts of the disjunction are false.

3. If the distributed antecedent term is placed in one proposition and its relative term in the other so that the distribution
of the one is not superimposed over the distribution of the
other, then it would not be unfitting to put the distributed
antecedent term in place of its relative term.

Si antecedens distributum ponitur in una propositione et relativum suum in alia, ita quod distributio unius non cadat
super distributionem alterius, tunc non esset inconveniens
loco relativi ponere suum antecedens distributum.

Instance: The proposition, Every man is running and the
same is eating, is equivalent with: Every man is running and
every man is eating. Since the antecedent is a copulative proposition, Albert is giving an instance of the valid thesis:

$$(x)[f(x) \cdot g(x)] \equiv [(x)f(x) \cdot (x)g(x)].$$

In connection with this rule he discusses certain difficulties
which are created by the possessive pronoun. For there is a vast
difference between saying: A donkey which belongs to every
man is running, and Of every man a donkey is running. In the
first case, at least one donkey would satisfy the proposition,
while, in the second proposition, there may be indicated at least
as many donkeys as there are men.

This rule and the instance of it, as likewise other instances, is,
in our opinion, a definitive proof that the scholastics had an idea
of two or even more quantifiers, and also of the position of the
quantifiers, if one is universal and the other particular. Using
the symbols D for "donkey", M for "man", P for "possessed

by" and R for "running", we can symbolize the first proposition (asinus cuiuslibet hominis currit) as follows:

$$\exists(y)\langle D(y) \cdot (x)[M(x) \supset P(y, x) \cdot R(y)]\rangle.$$

The second proposition: Cuiuslibet hominis asinus currit, could be made explicit in the following manner:

$$(x)\langle M(x) \supset \exists(y)[D(y) \cdot P(y, x) \cdot R(y)]\rangle.$$

V. Rules Concerning Ampliatio
(*Loc. cit.* cap. 10)

"Ampliatio" is defined by Albert as the acceptance of a term for some individual or individuals beyond the actually existing ones for which individual or individuals the term is denoted to be accepted in the proposition in which it occurs. The following rule is given.

1. Every term suppositing in reference to a verb of the past is amplified to supposit for that which has existed.
   Omnis terminus supponens respectu verbi de praeterito, ampliatur ad supponendum pro eo quod fuit.

Instance: Something white was something black. The term "white" in this proposition does not supposit for something that is white here and now. For this reason, such propositions are ambiguous, and the scholastics introduce the famous distinction: Such a term can supposit either for that which is or for that which was. The proposition will be true in one sense and false in the other sense.

VI. Rules Concerning Appellation
(*Loc. cit.* cap. 11)

Appellation is a property of the predicate. The technical term, appellation, means that the predicate has to be true, was true, or will be true, or can be true, etc., in its proper form. In other words, if the proposition is of the present, the proposition must be true, using the predicate, together with the present tense and a pronoun, as subject. For instance, Man is an animal. This proposition must be true in the form: This is an animal. If the proposition is of the past, then the proposition must have been true at some time in the past in its proper form. For instance, Something white was black. At a time in the past, it must have been true to say, pointing to that for which the subject stands: This is black. Similar rules are applied to propositions of the future and containing modalities.

These samples may suffice to give an idea of the highly developed theory of supposition.

NOTES

INTRODUCTION

1. We are not exaggerating by any means. In one of the most recent textbooks of neo-scholastic logic we read: "Logica tamen ipsius (Aristotelis) perfecta est: nihil ipsi addi potest, neque additum est in decursu saeculorum". [*Compendium Philosophiae Neo-Friburgensis Provinciae Brasiliae Centralis Societatis Jesu, volumen primum: Lo-. gica.* Auctore, P. Aloisio, G. Peixoto, Fortuna S.I., Nova Friburgo, Brasil, 1947, p. 27.] Of this remarkable statement, remarkable for its Kantian flavour, we give the following literal translation: "However, Aristotle's logic is perfect: nothing can be added to it, nor has anything been added to it during the course of centuries".

2. This seems to be also the opinion of Fr. I. M. Bochenski, O.P. We read in his recent article: "On the Categorical Syllogism", in *Dominican Studies*, I (1948), pp. 16 s.: "While all recent (Mathematical) Logicians continuously apply Formalism to all systems of Logic, all irrationalists and many idealists (as B. Croce) reject any use of it. Curiously enough, many eminent Thomists are following the irrationalists (as J. Maritain)." Again: "As a matter of fact, Formalism, which is one of the greatest inventions of Aristotle, has been the cause of considerable progress in Formal Logic, whenever it has been applied, e.g. by the Stoics, the Scholastics and the Mathematical Logicians".

3. These are amongst those being used in this country. The best of them is undoubtedly Jos. Gredt, O.S.B., *Elementa Philosophiae Aristo-telico-Thomisticae, Vol. 1: Logica, Philosophia Naturalis*, Friburgi Brisgoviae, 1937, We call it the best, since this logic has departed to lesser degree from the genuine logic of St. Thomas than any of the others.

4. This importance did not escape the attention of Aristotle himself. Cf. *On Sophistical Refutations*, c. 34; 183b 16 ss.

5. Cf. I. M. Bochenski, O.P., "Notiones Historiae Logicae Formalis", in *Angelicum*, 10 (1936), especially p. 110, concerning bibliographical notes. Lukasiewicz was the first to point at the historical importance of the Stoic logic in his article, "Zur Geschichte der Aussagenlogik", in *Erkenntnis*, 5 (1935), pp. 111-131.

6. Cf. Willard van Orman Quine, *Elementary Logic*, Ginn and Company, Boston, 1941, p. 166.

PART ONE

I. The Legacy of Scholastic Logic

7. Nostra intentio est, omnes dictas partes facere latinis intelligibiles. *Physic.*, lib. 1, tract. 1, c. 1; ed. Vivès, t. 3, p. 2a.

8. Cf. H. Scholz, *Geschichte der Logik*, Junker und Dünnhaupt, Berlin, 1931, pp. 22 ss.

9. Albert gives the following explanation of the title: . . . eo quod topos Graece est locus Latine: et id quod docetur in hoc libro, est qualiter ab habitudine locali trahatur consideratio ad problematis determinationem, *loc. cit.* p. 234a.

PART ONE

II. New Elements of Scholastic Logic

10. We hesitate to include here the tracts on the modes of signification, known as "De modis significandi" or "Grammatica speculativa", etc. Their topic is a rational discussion of the various significative functions of terms and their grammatical variations in the Latin language. In our opinion, their contribution to the development of logic seems to be of small importance. We do not dare call them studies in semantics, since they treat more and almost exclusively with a particular grammar. Information about semantics has to be sought in the commentaries on Aristotle's *Perihermenias* and in the tracts on the *Syncategoremata* and on supposition.

We might mention, in passing, that the necessity of developing new tracts in logic was felt by Albert himself. Cf. *Liber de praedicabilibus*, tract. 1, c. 5; ed. Vivès, p. 8: Istae ergo sunt duae partes logicae. Una quidem ut doceantur principia per quae sciatur definitio rei et quidditatis: ita quod per principia illa doceantur quae sit vera definitio, et quae non, et quae videatur esse et non sit. Alia vero ut doceantur principia qualiter per argumentationem probetur enuntiationis veritas vel falsitas. . . . Sed prima harum partium vel ab Antiquis tradita non est, vel ad nos non pervenit. Hanc etiam partem dicunt Avicenna et Alfarabius ad Arabes non pervenisse. Albert then gives a short outline of the desired tract's nature.

11. Cf. Reginald O'Donnell, C.S.B., "The Syncategoremata of William of Sherwood", in *Mediaeval Studies*, vol. 3, 1941, Pontifical Institute of Mediaeval Studies, pp. 46-93.

12. *Summa Logicae*, pars 1, c. 4. There are many editions of Ockham's work. We are using a text revised on the basis of several manuscripts of the early 14th century. For this reason we shall not quote any of the editions. The numbering of the chapters shows slight differences. Albert of Saxony, *Perutilis Logica*, tract. 1, c. 3; ed. Aurelius Sanutus, Venice, 1522. We shall use this text, revised, however, with the help of two manuscripts, viz. MS. Columbia University Library

(Plimpton Library) 143 and MS. Paris, Bibl. Nat. f. lat. 14715; both seem to be of the 14th century.

13. For further information we refer to G. Wallerand, *Les Œuvres de Siger de Courtrai*, in *Les Philosophes belges*, t. 8, Louvain, 1913, pp. (20) ss., and M. Grabmann, *Die Sophismenliteratur*.

14. We used two manuscripts, viz. Vat. lat. 3057 and Paris, Bibl. Nat. f. lat. 16134.

15. This Tractatus must not be confused either with the *Logica Moderna* (or *Modernorum*) or with the *Parva Logicalia*. In fact the *Logica Moderna*, if this title refers to a group of tracts and not to a general method used by the "modern logicians" of the Middle Ages, contains all the tracts which, in the Middle Ages, were considered to be new elements. These tracts in turn were sometimes united to the *Parva Logicalia* in works like *Copulata Tractatuum Logicalium*, which we know only in an incunabula edition. This document of the late Middle Ages gives the following explanation of the title *Parva Logicalia*:

Circa initium tractatuum parvorum logicalium quaeritur primo: Quot sint tractatus parvorum logicalium communiter legentium. Dicendum quod sex, scilicet suppositionum, ampliationum, appellationum, obligatoriorum, insolubilium et consequentiarum. Sed si absolute quaeratur, tunc sunt multo plures, scilicet distributionum, syncategorematum et exponibilium. Sed tantum isti sex in usu habentur. Ratio, quia sunt principaliores inter tractatus parvorum logicalium; etiam, quia ex istis quodammodo habetur cognitio aliorum: ut ex tractatu suppositionum aliqualiter cognoscuntur signa universalia et particularia, quorum natura traditur in tractatu distributionum et syncategorematum. . . . Sed quidam alii tractatus non habentur in usu propter eorum prolixitatem, ut sunt tractatus restrictionum et exponibilium.

The same unknown author also answers the question as to why these tracts are called *Parva Logicalia*. He gives four reasons: (1) They are treated in small books and presented in the form of tracts, whilst the works of Aristotle are offered in the style of "principal" books. (2) Only the principles of these tracts are laid down by Aristotle. Now, the principles, though few and concise, wield tremendous power. In relation, then, to the principles the tracts are called "small", that is, they are viewed as comparatively insignificant and of less moment. (3) They are concerned with the rudimentary elements, viz. with terms and their properties, which are the ultimate parts of the subject matter of logic. (4) These tracts are "small" in comparison with the other works composed by Peter of Spain. Note, however, that not all tracts dealt with in this little book of the anonymous author go back to Peter of Spain, as he erroneously seems to believe.

Ritter, "Studien zur Spätscholastik", in *Sitzungsberichte der Heidel-*

berger Akademie der Wissenschaften, Philosophisch - historische Klasse, Jahrgang 1922, 7. Abhandlung, Heidelberg, 1922, p. 89, footnote 1, rightly remarks concerning the *Parva Logicalia*: "Gewöhnlich: suppositio, ampliatio, appellatio, restrictio, distributio, exponibilia. Doch werden zu verschiedenen Zeiten noch verschiedene andere Teile zu den parva logicalia gerechnet, so bei Mars. von Inghen: alienatio, consequentiae."

16. William Shyreswood retains the distinction and carries it through in separate chapters. Cf. M. Grabmann, "Die Introductiones in logicam des Wilhelm von Shyreswood († nach 1267)", *Sitzungsberichte der Bayerischen Akademie der Wissenschaften*, Philosophisch-historische Abteilung, Jahrgang 1937, Heft 10, München, 1937, p. 81.

17. *Summulae Logicales* (with commentary of Dorp), tract. 4, *De appellationibus*; ed. Venice, 1499.

18. Cf., for instance, William Shyreswood, *Introductiones . . .*, ed. Grabmann (*op. cit.*, footnote 16), p. 83.

19. Cf. Cl. Baeumker, *Die "Impossibilia" des Sigers von Brabant*, in *Beiträge zur Geschichte der Philosophie des Mittelalters*, Bd. 2, Münster, 1898.

20. *Perutilis Logica*, tract. 6, c. 2; *ed. cit.*, fol. 47vb.

PART TWO

I. The Syncategoremata as Logical Constants

21. As to tracts on the *Syncategoremata* and other earlier tracts prior to Peter of Spain, see M. Grabmann, "Bearbeitungen und Auslegungen der Aristotelischen Logik aus der Zeit von Peter Abaelard bis Petrus Hispanus", in *Abhandlungen der Preussischen Akademie der Wissenschaften*, Philosophisch-historische Klasse, n. 5, Berlin, 1937.

22. Cf. the quotation from Priscian in O'Donnell's edition (*op. cit.*, footnote 11), p. 47. The editor is not convinced, however, that the "Stoics are meant. There seems no reason to believe it does not mean a dialectician as opposed to a grammarian even though Priscian goes on to speak of the Stoics" (*loc. cit.*).

23. There is a highly commendable unpretentious little book written by M. I. Bochenski, O.P., *Elementa Logicae Graecae*, Romae, 1937, which in the index identifies the "Dialectici" with the "Stoici".

24. The rather vague characterization of dependence of meaning or of degrees in the dependence or independence of meaning is hardly scholastic. R. Carnap, *Meaning and Necessity. A Study in Semantics* (The University of Chicago Press, Chicago, 1947, p. 7), rightly discards the degree of independence in meaning as an insufficient means to characterize syncategorematic terms and seems to minimize the importance of the distinction of terms into categorematic and syncategorematic terms. We concede his criticism, but we do not think that it concerns scholastic logic.

25. Cf. Ockham, *Summa Logicae*, pars I, c. 3, and *Quodlibeta*, v, q. 8; ed. Argentina. Cf. also our article: "Ockham's Theory of Signification", in *Franciscan Studies*, 6 (1946), pp. 152 s.

26. *Perutilis Logica*, tract. I, c. 3, fol. 2vb. Albert goes on to discuss the equivocation of certain terms which can be used either as pure syncategorematic terms or as categorematic terms, containing a syncategorematic term. For instance, the Latin word "aliquis", taken alone and as subject, is not a purely categorematic term, though it functions as such. The proposition: Aliquis currit, is to be translated: Some-*one* is running, which immediately brings out the categorematic content.

27. Tertia conclusio: Syncategorema non significat aliquam rem quae sit substantia vel accidens, sed bene significat modum rei, quod ab aliis vocatur significabile complexe. Patet hoc: nam praedicatum verificari de quolibet contento sub subiecto vel removeri a quolibet contento sub subiecto non est aliqua res quae sit substantia vel accidens, sed bene est modus rei et dispositio, puta subiecti vel praedicati. Et sic syncategorema bene significat aliquid, prout li aliquid non solum significat existentiam rei, sed etiam modum rei et caetera. *Quaestiones super Perihermenias*, edited in the *Expositio Aurea* of Ockham, ed. Bologna, 1496.

28. On the problem of the "significabile complexe" cf. Hubert Élie, *Le Complex significabile*, Paris, 1936, Vrin. Élie gives an interpretation different from that of Albert of Saxony.

29. Cf. *Burleus minor* of the Los Angeles MS. Univ. 6, first part. Albert of Saxony in his *Sophismata* follows a similar division of the Syncategoremata.

30. Albert of Saxony, *Perutilis Logica*, tract. 4, c. 1; fol. 24ra-b.

PART TWO

II. THE THEORY OF SUPPOSITION

31. For some historical notes on the origin of this doctrine see Joseph P. Mullally, *The Summulae Logicales of Peter of Spain, Publications in Medieval Studies*, vol. 8, Notre-Dame, 1945, pp. xxxviii ss.

32. Cf. Alexander of Hales, *Summa*, pars I, n. 364, 1-2; ed. Quaracchi, t. I, p. 540. There the editors refer to earlier scholastics. Cf. also *loc. cit.* n. 365 (p. 541), n. 390 (p. 574), and n. 402 (p. 591).

33. Cf. *Petri Hispani Summulae Logicales quas e codice manu scripto Reg. Lat. 1205 edidit I. M. Bochenski, O.P.*, Marietti, 1947, Torino, pp. xiv ss. There references to Grabmann are found.

34. Cf. ed. Bochenski, nn. 6.03-6.05; pp. 57 s.

35. *Op. cit.* (footnote 31), p. xlviii: "A substantive term possesses natural supposition when it is taken by itself. It is only when the term enters into a statement that it has accidental supposition."

36. Accidentalis suppositio est acceptio termini communis pro quibus

exigit adiunctum, ut "homo est"; iste terminus "homo" supponit hic pro praesentibus . . ., 6.04; p. 58. In contrast to it, natural supposition "est acceptio termini communis pro omnibus de quibus aptus natus est praedicari, ut 'homo' per se sumptus de natura sua habet suppositionem pro omnibus hominibus qui sunt et qui fuerunt et qui erunt". *loc. cit.*

37. Bochenski reads (6.05) "figurata"; Mullally (*ed. cit.* pp. 4, 59), however, "significata". We believe that the latter is correct, since, according to the older logicians and most of the realists in the Middle Ages, the spoken term signifies the "universal". Cf. William of Shyreswood, ed. Grabmann (footnote 21), p. 75.

38. We doubt whether "rational" in this sentence should be put within quotation marks. Mullally and Bochenski are correct in omitting them; Ockham, however, would have to add them, since, according to him, in this and the other sentences we are speaking about (mental) terms and are not using them.

39. Personalis suppositio est acceptio termini communis pro suis inferioribus, ut cum dicitur "homo currit", iste terminus "homo" supponit pro suis inferioribus, scilicet pro Socrate et Platone. Ed. Bochenski, 6.08.

40. The wording of the text is rather vague. For, when it is said: Confusa autem suppositio est acceptio termini communis pro pluribus mediante signo universali (6.10), it seems thereby excluded that such a term might stand for only one individual. According to Shyreswood (ed. Grabmann, p. 83), an affirmative proposition with the sign "omnis" attached to the subject demands at least three individuals as suppositis. Peter of Spain rejects this view, however. Cf. 12.09 ss.

41. Cf. the discussions in 6.11-6.22.

42. This distinction was, of course, known prior to Ockham.

43. *Summa Logicae*, pars 1, c. 62. For further information cf. our article: "Ockham's Theory of Supposition and the Notion of Truth", in *Franciscan Studies*, 6 (1946), pp. 262 ss.

44. *Summa Logicae*, pars 1, c. 76.

45. *Loc. cit.* c. 1.

46. *Loc. cit.* c. 67.

47. *Loc. cit.* c. 66.

48. *Loc. cit.* cc. 68 and 69; also for the following.

49. Est igitur regula certa, quod quando sub termino communi contingit descendere ad singularia per propositionem disiunctivam, et ex qualibet singulari infertur talis propositio, tunc ille terminus habet suppositionem personalem determinatam. *loc. cit.* c. 68.

50. Cf. ed. Bochenski, 6.17.

51. This addition is necessary, as Ockham is aware, since he and most of the medieval logicians admit that, for instance, the proposition: "Omnis Phoenix est", is correct, though it is supposed that there is but one individual bird which is a Phoenix.

52. MS. Erfurt, *Amploniana* o.67, fol. 123b (recent numeration): Hanc extractionem de logica Burle ordinavit frater Johannes Nicholai lector de custodia lincopnensi (?) provinciae daciae, quando studuit Parisiis anno Domini M°CCC°XXIX°, de cuius logicae commendatione praemisit prologum in hunc modum: Post praecedentem summam editam a fratre W(ilhelmo) compilavit Burle alium tractatum de logica in quo pauca continentur utilia realiter nihil vel sumpta de priori summa vel de Boecio in libro de categoricis et hypotheticis syllogismis. Quae tamen in ipso iudicavi esse utilia posita ultra ea quae posita in summa praecedenti vel quae sunt contra ea quae dicuntur in illa summa, ut opposita iuxta se posita marginaliter elucescant melius, breviter in sequentibus colliguntur.

53. Cf. the "Incipit" of the tract: Suppositis significatis terminorum complexorum in hoc tractatu intendo perscrutari de quibusdam proprietatibus terminorum, quae solum eis competunt secundum quod sunt partes propositionis. Et hunc tractatum divido in tres partes: Prima est de suppositione terminorum, secunda est de appellatione, et tertia de copulatione. Suppositio debetur subiecto, appellatio praedicato, et copulatio debetur verbo copulanti praedicatum cum subiecto. Ista enim tria sunt partes integrantes propositionem categoricam.

54. Suppositio proprie dicta est proprietas termini subiecti ad praedicatum comparati. Et sumitur hic terminus pro quolibet indifferenter, quod potest esse extremum propositionis, sive sit terminus simplex sive aggregatum ex adiectivo et substantivo, sive etiam sit compositum mediante copulatione vel disiunctione.

55. Burleigh tells us that he intends to present only a few of the many divisions that he used to give in his earlier years: Plurimas divisiones in iuventute mea inveni me scripsisse, sed in praesenti opusculo nolo tot membra ponere, quia ad praesens propositum sufficiunt pauciora.

56. Et dicitur materialis, quando ipsa dictio supponit vel pro ipsa voce absoluta vel pro ipsa dictione composita ex voce et significatione, ut si dicamus: Homo est dissyllabum, Homo est nomen. Ed. Grabmann, p. 75.

57. Suppositio materialis est, quando vox supponit pro seipsa vel pro alia voce quae non est inferior ad illam.

58. Burleigh objects against Ockham's theory of signification: Sed sine dubio illud est valde irrationabiliter dictum, salva gloria eorum; nam in ista: Homo est species, secundum quod est vera, iste terminus homo supponit pro significato. . . . After having offered several proofs from reason and authorities he continues: Ideo dico, sicut dicere consuevi, quod quando terminus communis vel terminus concretus singularis vel singulare aggregatum supponit pro eo, quod significat, quod tunc habet suppositionem simplicem. . . .

59. Quando terminus communis supponit pro suppositis vel terminus

aggregatus supponit pro termino simplici de quo accidentaliter praedicatur, tunc habet suppositionem personalem.

60. Cf. *op. cit.* (footnote 3), p. 43.

PART TWO

III. THE THEORY OF CONSEQUENCES

61. Cf. "De consequentiis scholasticorum earumque origine", in *Angelicum*, 15 (1938), pp. 92-109. There are also references to works of Lukasiewicz and Salamucha. We disagree with Bochenski in so far as he does not mention the *Topics of Aristotle* as the main starting-point of the scholastic consequences, although he does not deny the importance of their relation to a few of Aristotle's scattered remarks which are enumerated by the author on page 107. We should like to emphasize that we are speaking of the historical, not of the logical starting-point.

62. Sed quia conditionalis aequivalet uni consequentiae, ita quod tunc conditionalis est vera, quando antecedens infert consequens, et non aliter, ideo differatur usque ad tractatum de consequentiis. . . . Est etiam sciendum, quod ad veritatem conditionalis nec requiritur veritas antecedentis nec consequentis, immo est aliquando conditionalis necessaria et quaelibet pars eius est impossibilis, sicut hic: Si Sortes est asinus, est rudibilis. *Summa Logicae*, pars 2, c. 30.

63. Consequentia ut nunc est, quando antecedens pro aliquo tempore potest esse verum sine consequente, sed non pro isto tempore. *Op. cit.* partis 3, pars 3, c. 1.

64. Consequentia simplex est, quando pro nullo tempore poterit antecedens esse verum sine consequente. *loc. cit.*

65. Illa consequentia tenet per medium intrinsecum, quando tenet per aliquam propositionem formatam ex eisdem terminis sicut ista: Sortes non currit, igitur homo non currit, tenet virtute istius medii: Sortes est homo . . . et per talia media tenent syllogismi omnes. *loc. cit.*

66. Consequentia autem, quae tenet per medium extrinsecum est, quando tenet per aliquam regulam generalem quae non plus respicit illos terminos quam alios. *loc. cit.*

67. Consequentia formalis est duplex, quia quaedam tenet per medium extrinsecum quod respicit formam propositionis, sicut sunt tales regulae: Ab exclusiva ad universalem de terminis transpositis est consequentia bona; Ex maiore de necessario et minore de inesse sequitur conclusio de necessario, et huiusmodi. Quaedam tenet per medium intrinsecum immediate et mediate per medium extrinsecum respiciens generales conditiones propositionum, non veritatem nec falsitatem nec necessitatem nec impossibilitatem, cuiusmodi est ista: Sortes non currit, igitur homo non currit. *loc. cit.*

68. Consequentia materialis est, quando tenet ratione terminorum praecise, et non ratione alicuius medii extrinseci respicientis praecise generales conditiones propositionum, cuiusmodi sunt tales: Si homo currit, Deus est; Homo est asinus, igitur Deus non est, et huiusmodi. *loc. cit.*

69. Cf. C. I. Lewis and C. H. Langford, *Symbolic Logic*, The Century Co., New York and London, 1932, p. 86.

70. We have profited by Salamucha's treatment of the Consequences of Ockham. However, we shall depart occasionally from his symbolization and interpretation, since we have to take care not to interpret every consequential rule as a material consequence. In fact, most of the rules regard formal consequences. It is of course true that every formal consequence holds as material consequence, though not vice versa.

71. *Summa Logicae*, partis 3, pars 3, c. 36.

72. Et ideo, quando antecedens est verum et consequens falsum, consequentia non valet; et haec est ratio sufficiens ad probandum consequentiam non valere. *loc. cit.*

73. Notandum est hic, quod semper quando est una consequentia, si sit fallacia consequentis, non tenet consequentia, sed e converso bene sequitur. Quoted from the still inedited *Expositio super libros Elenchorum*, lib. 2, ad: *Illos qui per consequens. . . .*

74. Sciendum est, quod antecedens est totum quod praecedit consequens. Et ideo aliquando antecedens est tantum una propositio, et aliquando continet plures propositiones, sicut patet in syllogismo. Et tunc, quamvis una illarum propositionum sit vera, conclusio poterit esse falsa; sed si quaelibet illarum fuerit vera, non poterit conclusio esse falsa, si sequitur ex eis. *Summa Logicae, loc. cit.*

75. *Loc. cit.*

76. *Loc. cit.*

77. . . . ita quod si consequens sit falsum, oportet quod totum antecedens sit falsum vel quod aliqua propositio, quae est pars antecedentis, sit falsa; sed non oportet quod quaelibet propositio quae est pars antecedentis sit falsa: quin aliquando ex una propositione vera et alia falsa sequitur conclusio falsa, sicut patet hic: Omnis homo est animal, lapis est homo, igitur lapis est animal. *loc. cit.*

78. *Loc. cit.*

79. Notandum est, quod quando antecedens est una propositio, semper, si sit consequentia bona, ex opposito consequentis sequitur oppositum totius antecedentis; sed quando antecedens continet plures propositiones, tunc non oportet quod ex opposito consequentis sequitur oppositum cuiuslibet propositionis quae est antecedens. . . . *loc. cit.*

80. *Loc. cit.*

81. *Loc. cit.*

82. *Loc. cit.*

83. *Summa Logicae*, partis 3, pars 1, c. 6.

84. *Summa Logicae*, partis 3, pars 3, c. 36.

85. Ex ista regula sequitur alia, scilicet quidquid antecedit ad antecedens antecedit ad consequens: quia aliter aliquid sequeretur ad consequens quod non sequeretur ad antecedens. Sed istae regulae falsae
sunt: Quicquid sequitur ad antecedens, sequitur ad consequens; nam
sequitur: Omne animal currit, igitur omnis homo currit; et tamen
non sequitur: Omnis asinus currit, igitur omnis homo currit. Similiter ista regula est falsa: Quidquid antecedit ad consequens, antecedit ad antecedens, propter idem. *loc. cit.*

86. Hence we do not take "consistency" in the sense of Lewis-Langford,
op. cit. pp. 153 s. According to the authors a true conjunction strictly
implies the consistency of the members of the conjunction, not, however, vice versa.

87. Sed non quidquid stat cum consequente stat cum antecedente; nam
cum isto consequente: Omnis homo currit, stat ista: Aliquis asinus
non currit: et tamen non stat cum ista antecedente: Omne animal
currit, et hoc quando antecedens non sequitur ad consequens, nec
consequentia simplici, nec consequentia ut nunc. *loc. cit.*

88. *Loc. cit.*

89. *Summa Logicae*, pars 2, c. 32.

90. *Loc. cit.*

91. Tamen sciendum, quod quandoque ab altera parte copulativae ad
copulativam potest esse consequentia bona gratia materiae, puta si
una pars copulativae infert aliam, tunc ab illa ad totam copulativam
est consequentia bona. *loc. cit.*

92. Disiunctiva est illa, quae componitur ex pluribus categoricis mediante hac coniunctione vel mediante aliquo aequivalente sibi. . . .
Ad veritatem autem disiunctivae requiritur, quod altera pars sit
vera. . . . *op. cit.* c. 33.

93. *Loc. cit.*

94. Et idem sufficit et requiritur ad veritatem oppositae disiunctivae,
quod sufficit et requiritur ad veritatem copulativae. *loc. cit.*

95. *Loc. cit.*

96. *Perutilis Logica*, tract. 3, c. 5.

97. *Summa Logicae, loc. cit.*

98. *Perutilis Logica*, tract. 4, c. 1.

99. Propositio vera est illa, quae qualitercumque significat, ita est. Propositio autem falsa est illa quae non qualitercumque significat, ita
est. *op. cit.*, tract. 3, c. 3.

100. We shall present here a revised text of the pertinent passage without further comment: Sed contra: Si consequens impossibile est esse
verum, tunc consequens est impossibile, et sic ex possibili sequitur
impossibile, quod est falsum. Respondetur negando consequentiam:
Consequens est impossibile esse verum, ergo consequens est impossibile. Unde multa sunt possibilia quae tamen impossibile est esse
vera. . . . Similiter ista existens in mente Sortis: Sortes non est, est

possibilis, quia eius contradictoria non est necessaria, scilicet: Sortes est; et tamen impossibile est eam esse veram, quia quamdiu est, ipsa est falsa, quando autem non est, ipsa non est vera. Nam quamdiu ipsa est: Sortes est, ex quo ponitur esse in mente Sortis, et quamdiu est, ipsa est falsa. Unde finaliter concedo, quod aliquid possibile impossibile est esse verum; aliud est enim dicere, aliquid esse impossibile, et ipsum impossibile esse verum. *loc. cit.*

101. Consequentia autem est propositio hypothetica composita ex antecedente et consequente et nota consequentiae significans antecedens esse antecedens et consequens esse consequens. *loc. cit.*

102. Consequentiae autem ut nunc vocantur, quae simpliciter loquendo non sunt bonae, quia possibile est sic esse sicut significat antecedens sine hoc quod sit sic sicut significat consequens; sed sunt bonae ut nunc, quia impossibile est rebus se habentibus, ut nunc se habent, sic esse, sicut significat antecedens, quin sit sic, sicut significat consequens. Et istis consequentiis vulgariter saepe utimur (*Philosophus saepe utitur*, MS. Columbia Univ.). Verbi gratia, ut si dicamus: Sortes currit, ergo magister in artibus currit, supposito quod Sortes sit magister in artibus. Et ista consequentia reducitur ad consequentiam formalem per additionem alicuius propositionis verae, non tamen necessariae, vel aliquarum verarum, non tamen necessariarum. Verbi gratia: Sortes currit, Sortes est magister in artibus, ergo magister in artibus currit. *loc. cit.*

103. Consequentiae simpliciter vocantur quae simpliciter sunt bonae et sic se habent quod non est possibile sic esse sicut significat antecedens, quin sit sic, sicut significat consequens. *loc. cit.*

PART THREE
Systems of Scholastic Logic

104. Cf. Mullally, *op. cit.* pp. 133-158.

105. Cf. Bochenski, *Summulae Logicales, ed. cit.* p. xv.

106. As, for instance, William Shyreswood, Lambert of Auxerre and Buridan.

107. Cf. the beginning of the *Summa Logicae*: Omnes Logicae tractatores intendunt astruere, quod argumenta et syllogismi ex propositionibus et propositiones ex terminis componuntur.

108. Because of the historical importance of this passage we shall edit here the Latin text: Dicto de regulis generalibus omnis consequentiae dicenda sunt aliqua specialia consequentiae syllogisticae. Dico igitur, quod duae sunt regulae generales omni syllogismo in quacumque figura vel modo fiat, scilicet quod habeat alteram propositionem universalem et alteram affirmativam, quia ex negativa nihil sequitur syllogistice nec ex particulari.

Praeter istas regulas communes omni figurae sunt quaedam regulae speciales in qualibet figura. In prima figura sunt duae regulae scilicet quod in modis concludentibus directe maior debet esse universalis, et minor affirmativa.

In secunda figura sunt aliae regulae. Una, scilicet quod maior debet esse universalis, et altera negativa.

In tertia vero sunt aliae regulae, scilicet quod minor semper sit affirmativa et conclusio particularis. Si alio modo fiat, non valet syllogismus.

Haec quae dicta sunt de consequentiis sufficiant.

NOTES TO APPENDIX I

1. In order to express the character of a sophisma we did not add any comma. We shall use the following symbols: P for: All men are donkeys, Q for: All men are men, R for: Donkeys are donkeys, S for: Men are donkeys.
2. $(P \vee Q) \cdot R$. In ordinary language: All men are donkeys or all men are men, and donkeys are donkeys.
3. $P \vee (S \cdot R)$. In ordinary language: All men are donkeys, or men are donkeys and donkeys are donkeys.
4. Viz. the sign "all".
5. Viz. where Albert discusses sophismata, owing their difficulty to signs of quantification.
6. Viz.: Every proposition or its contradictory opposite is true.
7. The well-known theorem: $(p \cdot q) \supset p$ and: $(p \cdot q) \supset q$.
8. Another theorem: $p \supset (p \vee q)$ and: $q \supset (p \vee q)$.
9. $p \supset (p \vee \bar{p})$.
10. Viz. of the consequent: $\overline{p \vee \bar{p}}$.
11. $p \vee \bar{p} \equiv \overline{\bar{p} \cdot p}$.
12. Viz. $(p \cdot \bar{p}) \supset \bar{p}$.
13. The theorem: $(\bar{q} \supset \bar{p}) \supset (p \supset q)$.
14. A negative disjunctive proposition would be of the type: $\overline{p \vee q}$.
15. Hence this is false: $\bar{p} \supset p \vee \bar{p}$.
16. Viz. the contradiction of $p \vee \bar{p}$ is: $\overline{p \vee \bar{p}}$.
17. The theorem: $[(p \vee q) \cdot \bar{p}] \supset q$ and likewise for q.
18. $(p \cdot \bar{p}) \supset q$.
19. $(p \supset q) \supset [(q \supset r) \supset (p \supset r)]$.
20. That is of the antecedent.
21. In symbolization: $(p \cdot \bar{p}) \supset p$.
22. Viz. $p \supset (p \vee q)$.
23. Hence we obtain: $[(p \cdot \bar{p}) \supset p] \supset \langle [p \supset (p \vee q)] \supset [(p \cdot \bar{p}) \supset (p \vee q)] \rangle$.
    Since both the antecedent of the entire consequence and the consequence in the consequent are asserted, it follows: $(p \cdot \bar{p}) \supset (p \vee q)$.

24. $(p \cdot \bar{p}) \supset \bar{p}$.

25. $(p \cdot \bar{p}) \supset [(p \vee q) \cdot \bar{p}]$.

26. The theorem (footnote 17).

27. Viz.: All men are donkeys, and also: Men and donkeys are donkeys.

28. The ambiguity is patent, if we symbolize either $\bar{p} \vee q$ or $\overline{p \vee q}$.

29. $\bar{p} \vee q$ where q is true.

30. $p \vee q$.

31. $p \vee \bar{q}$.

32. $\bar{p} \vee q$.

33. $\bar{p} \vee q \equiv \overline{p \cdot \bar{q}}$ which means that $p \cdot q$ contradicts $\bar{p} \vee q$.

INDEX OF PROPER NAMES

www.ingramcontent.com/pod-product-compliance
Lightning Source LLC
Chambersburg PA
CBHW060354090426
42734CB00011B/2132